RECLAIMING WISDOM

TRANSFORMING EDUCATION FOR A CONSCIOUS FUTURE

AINDRILA GHOSAL

To my first teachers, my parents, who have taught me to be a lifelong learner, to stay humble in knowledge, and to embrace a growth mindset. Everything I am, I owe to your wisdom and love.

To my husband and mentor, Subhradip, whose guidance, encouragement, and unwavering support have been the pillars of my journey. Without you, my life would have been meaningless and this journey would have not been possible.

And to the teachings of Swami Vivekananda and Rabindranath Tagore, whose words have shaped my understanding of life, learning, and spirituality. This book is, in many ways, a reflection of the wisdom they have passed down to the world.

With deepest gratitude.

Contents

Preface — vii

Chapter Insights — xi

1. THE PURPOSE OF EDUCATION – A JOURNEY BEYOND KNOWLEDGE — 1

2. EDUCATION AS A PATH TO CONSCIOUS EVOLUTION — 18

3. MASLOW'S HIERARCHY OF NEEDS: A PSYCHOLOGICAL FRAMEWORK FOR GROWTH IN EDUCATION — 43

4. BLOOM'S TAXONOMY AND INTELLECTUAL EVOLUTION — 60

5. THE NEED FOR A HOLISTIC APPROACH TO EDUCATION — 85

6. EDUCATION AS A PATH TO HIGHER CONSCIOUSNESS — 98

7. CONCLUSION, Or Is It? — 110

Author's Note — 115

About The Author — 117

Citations and Sources — 119

Preface

What if I told you that the education system you and I have been a part of for generations was never designed to awaken minds, but to control them? That the structure we accept today—grades, exams, rote learning, and mechanical skill-building—is not a natural evolution of human intelligence but a system imposed upon us to strip away independent thought and replace it with blind obedience?

This is not an exaggeration. It is history.

There was a time when India was home to the most advanced education system in the world—the Gurukul tradition, where learning was not confined to textbooks but was a lived experience. Students didn't just memorize theories; they observed, questioned, debated, and realized. Education was not about producing workers; it was about creating enlightened human beings, about shaping individuals who could think beyond themselves, who could see beyond the illusion of the material world, and who could rise above conditioned existence.

But all of that changed.

The British colonial system of education was not built to create visionaries; it was built to manufacture clerks, bureaucrats, and subordinates—individuals who would serve the empire, not question it. Lord Macaulay's infamous 1835 education policy systematically erased India's wisdom traditions, replacing them with a rigid, Westernized model that valued compliance over curiosity, utility over wisdom, and memorization over true learning. What started as a colonial project to weaken a civilization has, over time, become our own accepted reality, a cycle we continue to follow without questioning its origins.

And now, as we step into the era of Artificial Intelligence, another storm is upon us.

AI can now write essays, solve equations, compose music, and even generate philosophical arguments. With just a few prompts, it can do in seconds what human beings have spent lifetimes mastering. This raises a terrifying question: If education is merely about acquiring knowledge, and AI can do that better than us, then what is the purpose of human learning at all?

This book is an urgent call to reclaim what we have lost before it is too late. It is a call to break free from an outdated, colonized model of education and embrace an approach that is not just about knowing but about becoming. It is a call to return to the wisdom of our past, not as a rejection of modernity, but as a way to redefine our future.

Through this book, we will explore:

- The ancient Gurukul system and how it nurtured holistic, wisdom-based learning instead of exam-based conditioning.
- The teachings of Swami Vivekananda and Rabindranath Tagore, who fought against the colonized education system and envisioned a model that encouraged creativity, self-inquiry, and consciousness.
- The crisis of modern education in the age of AI and why our schools and universities are failing to prepare students for a world where machines can outperform them in everything except wisdom.
- Gurdjieff's philosophy on breaking free from unconscious learning, and how we must evolve beyond mechanical existence into true intellectual and spiritual awakening.

This book is not just for educators, policymakers, or intellectuals. It is for anyone who has ever felt that something is missing in our education system. It is for every student who has memorized pages of information but never been taught how to think, every teacher who feels trapped by a rigid syllabus instead of being allowed to inspire, and every parent who knows that their child's intelligence is worth more than just a report card.

We are at a pivotal moment in history. If we do not change the way we educate now, we may lose our last opportunity to shape the next generation into conscious, awakened individuals. AI will continue to evolve, technology will continue to replace human tasks, but wisdom cannot be coded into an algorithm. The question is—will we rise to the challenge and reclaim education's true purpose, or will we allow it to be reduced to something machines can do better than us?

This book is not just a critique—it is a manifesto for change. It is a wake-up call, a challenge, and an invitation to rethink everything we believe about learning. Because education was never meant to be about filling minds. It was always meant to be about awakening them.

And now, it is up to us to decide—will we continue sleepwalking through an outdated system, or will we finally open our eyes?

Chapter Insights

1. Introduction

- The Purpose of Education
- Gurdjieff's Vision of Human Evolution
- Why Education Must Be More Than Information Transfer

2. Education as a Path to Conscious Evolution

- Why Education needs to deliberately evolve
- Gurdjieff-Maslow-Bloom-Indian Philosophy: Modern Education and the crisis of Un-awakened learning
- Historical vs. Modern-Day Examples

3. Maslow's Hierarchy of Needs: A Psychological Framework for Growth in Education

- Physiological to Self-Actualization: A Parallel with Gurdjieff and Indian Philosophies
- Old Education vs. Modern Education
- Reevaluating Maslow: Why Indian Philosophies Offer a More Complete Path to Human Growth

4. *Bloom's Taxonomy and Intellectual Evolution*

- The Progession of Learning
- The Indian Perspective on Intellectual Evolution: Kosha System
- Beyond Bloom's Taxonomy

5. *The Need for a Holistic Approach to Education*

- Bridging Intellectual, Emotional, and Spiritual Growth
- Experiential Learning and Self-Inquiry
- The Role of Teachers in Awakening Consciousness
- Teaching as a Path to Awakening

6. *Education as a Path to Higher Consciousness*

- The Forgotten Purpose of Learning in the Age of AI
- The Gurukul System and Wisdom Traditions
- The Need for a Return to Ancient Knowledge in the Age of AI

7. *Conclusion, Or Is it?*

- A Call for Change - From Shikshaks to Gurus
- A New Model of Education for the Future
- Education Beyond Knowledge: Role of Educators

THE PURPOSE OF EDUCATION – A JOURNEY BEYOND KNOWLEDGE

Introduction: The Lost Meaning of Education

There is an old saying in the Upanishads:

"Sa Vidya Ya Vimuktaye" – True knowledge is that which liberates.

But what does it mean to be liberated?

The word education is derived from the Latin educare, meaning *to draw out* or *to bring forth*. It implies that knowledge is not something to be forcefully inserted into a person, but rather something innate that must be awakened. Yet, in today's world, education has been reduced to memorization, rote learning, and competition. Instead of helping individuals awaken to their true nature, it traps them in a mechanical existence, detached from self-awareness and inner wisdom.

Let's understand how it used to be:

Once upon a time, in a small village on the banks of the Saraswati River, a young boy named Manu sat under the shade of an ancient banyan tree. His Guru, who was a wise sage, asked him:

"Manu, what do you seek?"

The boy hesitated before answering, *"I seek knowledge."*

The sage smiled, *"But what will you do with knowledge?"*

Manu thought for a moment. *"I will pass my tests, become a scholar, and earn respect."*

The Guru's smile deepened. *"And then?"*

Manu fell silent.

The Guru then placed a hand on his shoulder. *"Knowledge that does not lead to wisdom is like a lamp that burns in an empty room—bright but useless. True knowledge awakens the soul, not just the mind."*

This was the education of ancient India—a journey of self-realization rather than blind accumulation of facts.

Now, fast forward to the present, and we meet Manas, a bright but exhausted student preparing for his board exams in an elite international school. His life is a whirlwind of tuition classes, revision schedules, and sleepless nights. His parents are anxious about his future, and are pushing him to score perfect grades because in their eyes, his entire life depends on his marks.

Unlike Manu, Manas has never been asked, *"What do you seek?"* He has never wondered whether knowledge has a deeper purpose beyond securing a job and financial stability. He is part of a system that produces intelligent but disconnected individuals, those who are academically brilliant but spiritually empty.

The two boys—one from the past, one from the present—represent two different paradigms of education. One nurtures consciousness; the other nurtures careers. One aims for awakening, while the other aims for productivity.

But the question is, what is the true purpose of education?

Gurdjieff's Vision of Human Evolution: Why Education Must Be More Than Information

1.1 The Sleeping Man and the Illusion of Learning

The Russian-Armenian mystic G.I. Gurdjieff (c. 1866–1877) saw human beings as existing in a state of sleep, trapped in habitual patterns, mechanical thinking, and conditioned responses. He believed that most people go through life without ever truly waking up—their thoughts, actions, and beliefs dictated by external influences rather than by conscious choice. To him, education, in its highest form, was not about acquiring information but about breaking free from this state of unconscious existence and evolving into a fully awakened being.

If we are to understand the true purpose of learning, we must first understand why Gurdjieff insisted that human evolution is not automatic—that without deliberate effort, we remain stagnant, repeating the same cycles. This idea challenges everything we have been taught about education. We assume that accumulating knowledge makes us more evolved, but does it? Can memorization, degrees, and skills alone bring true understanding, or is there something deeper we must seek?

In this section, let's first explore how Gurdjieff's philosophy compels us to redefine education, to see it not as a system that merely imparts knowledge, but as a transformative process that awakens the intellect, refines emotional intelligence, and ultimately leads to self-mastery. Without this shift in perspective, education will remain a cycle of conditioned learning, producing individuals who may be intelligent but not truly aware.

Gurdjieff categorized humanity into seven levels of consciousness, or seven types of "Man"—each representing a different stage of self-awareness and evolution.

- Man-1: Lives purely through physical impulses, ruled by instincts.
- Man-2: Dominated by emotions, acting out of likes and dislikes.
- Man-3: Functions through intellect but lacks deeper wisdom.
- Man-4: Begins to awaken, seeking balance between mind, heart, and body.
- Man-5: Achieves true self-awareness, mastering thoughts and emotions.
- Man-6: Transcends ego, living with profound purpose and harmony.
- Man-7: The fully realized being—like a Buddha or a Krishna—who has awakened completely.

These levels eerily mirror the spiritual progression described in Indian scriptures. The Vedas and Upanishads describe the journey of a seeker from being *Avidya* (ignorant) to *Vidya* (enlightened). In the Bhagavad Gita, Krishna repeatedly tells Arjun that the greatest battle is not fought on the battlefield but within one's own consciousness.

Yet, modern education remains stuck in the lower levels of human evolution, focusing only on intellectual achievements rather than holistic development.

1.2 Education Through Gurdjieff's Lens: A Journey from Mechanical Learning to Conscious Growth

In our modern classrooms, students arrive like blank slates, waiting to be filled with facts, formulas, and theories. They sit in neat rows, absorb information, and regurgitate it in exams. Success is measured in grades, ranks, and college acceptances, not in wisdom, self-awareness, or true understanding.

If we take a deeper dig at Gurdjieff's philosophy, this system would have been seen as deeply flawed as this is a mere mechanical process that produces more sleepwalkers than awakened beings. In his view, most people exist at the level of Man-1 (instinctive),

Man-2 (emotional), and Man-3 (intellectual), but true education should lead them towards Man-4 (self-aware), Man-5 (awakened), and beyond.

But how does one awaken education from this deep sleep?

The question still stands, and in order to understand the answer, let us explore this question through three fundamental failings of modern education, as seen through Gurdjieff's model, and understand how they can be transformed into paths toward higher consciousness.

a. The Mechanical Student: Learning Without Awareness

Let's look at this first scenario. We are looking at a prestigious international school in Mumbai, where a young girl named Ishita spends her days memorizing textbooks. She is an ideal student—scoring perfect grades, winning academic prizes, and earning admiration from teachers.

Yet, deep inside, Ishita fells hollow. She is not truly learning—she is merely absorbing and repeating. She could solve complex calculus problems, but she struggles to make sense of her own emotions. She could write perfect essays, but she has no idea what she truly believed.

One day, after securing the highest score in her final exams, Ishita's father took her out for dinner.

"Beta, I am so proud of you," he said. *"With these scores, you will get into the Ivy Leagues for sure."*

Ishita smiled, but inside, she felt a strange sense of emptiness.

Ishita here, represents Man-3 in Gurdjieff's model—the intellectual man, deeply trained in logic and reason but completely disconnected from self-awareness. Education, instead of leading her towards wisdom, had turned her into a mechanical learner, an automaton.

Now, let's compare this with education in ancient India, where a young student, Uddalaka, once sat before his Guru in the forest. His teacher did not give him a book filled with facts. Instead, he asked him a question:

"What is the essence of all things?"

Uddalaka was confused. He gave many answers—fire, air, water—but his teacher shook his head. Finally, after years of deep contemplation, the student realized the profound truth:

"Tat Tvam Asi—You Are That."

The difference is staggering. Modern education fills students with information but does not teach them to seek truth for themselves. It trains them to answer questions but does not teach them to ask the right ones.

What should be done? - Breaking Free from Mechanical Learning

Shifting students from Man-3, the state of mechanical intelligence, to Man-4, the realm of self-awareness, requires a fundamental rethinking of education. Learning cannot remain a passive act of memorization; it must become an active process of questioning, analyzing, and seeking deeper understanding. When students blindly accept information, they remain trapped in conditioned thought, never truly engaging with the world around them. A classroom should not be a space where teachers dictate answers, but one where Socratic dialogue flourishes, where students are challenged to think for themselves, to debate, and to arrive at conclusions through guided exploration. True learning happens through experience, through direct interaction with the world, where knowledge is not just absorbed but lived, tested, and internalized. Education should no longer be about producing individuals who simply excel in exams; it must awaken seekers—those who think, question, and evolve beyond the limits of mechanical intelligence.

b. *The Emotional Student: Learning Through Fear and Reward*

Now let's look at Rohan, a boy from Delhi, who had always been an anxious child. His school life was defined by fear of failure. He studied not because he loved learning, but because he feared disappointment, punishment, and shame.

One day, his teacher announced, *"There will be a surprise test tomorrow."*

Needless to say, Rohan's heart raced. He could already imagine his mother's disappointed face, his father's scolding, the shame of scoring less than his classmates.

That night, he crammed his textbooks, barely sleeping. The next day, he vomited from stress before entering the classroom.

Rohan represents Man-2 (emotional man) in Gurdjieff's model—a person whose learning is driven not by curiosity, but by emotional conditioning. Such students do not engage with knowledge freely; they associate it with stress, fear, and societal pressure.

Now, let's contrast this with the Gurukul system of education. Unlike the rigid, exam-driven education system of today, the ancient Gurukul system was rooted in patience, trust, and inner joy, allowing learning to flourish as a natural process rather than a forced one. A student was not pressured by the fear of failure, the weight of materialistic competition, or the burden of external validation. Instead, the Guru served as a guide, not an enforcer, recognizing that fact that true understanding cannot be rushed as it must emerge organically, much like a seed growing into a tree. Curiosity was not suppressed under the weight of syllabi; it was nurtured, encouraged, and expanded upon. The Guru's role was to cultivate an environment where learning was joyful, knowledge was absorbed through experience, and wisdom was not dictated but discovered. There was no concept of rote memorization or mindless repetition; instead, learning was a dialogue between teacher and student, a process of inner realization. There was the

Shruti and *Smriti* tradition; however, it too followed an inquiry-based dialogue format. Education was not considered to be a race toward an exam date but a lifelong journey toward self-discovery, where knowledge blossomed effortlessly, like a flower opening to the warmth of the sun.

What should be done? - Healing Emotional Learning

Students trapped in Man-2, the stage of emotionally conditioned learning, absorb knowledge through the lens of fear—fear of failure, fear of judgment, fear of falling behind. Education, when driven by fear, stifles curiosity and turns learning into a burden rather than a journey. Instead of instilling anxiety, classrooms must become spaces of exploration, where students are free to fail without punishment and succeed without pressure. Learning should not be a desperate race for approval but a deeply intrinsic pursuit, where students see knowledge as something to uncover, question, and integrate into their own understanding of the world. Mindfulness must become an essential part of education, teaching students to process emotions rather than be controlled by them. Fear has always been the greatest enemy of learning—when it dissolves, curiosity thrives, and true education finally begins.

c. The Instinctive Student: The Prison of Habitual Learning

Now, let's shift our attention towards Raj. Raj hails from a small town in Madhya Pradesh. He was an average student, never excelling but never failing. He followed the same routine every day—wake up, go to school, copy notes, take exams, and repeat. He never questioned anything, never thought deeply, never explored beyond what was required.

He was, in Gurdjieff's terms, Man-1—the instinctive man, who learns not through intellect or emotion, but through mechanical habit.

For him, education was not an awakening experience, but an endless cycle of repetition.

This is the reality of most students today. They move through the system like factory workers on an assembly line, shaped by syllabuses, standardized tests, and predictable routines.

Now let's compare this story with that of Nachiketa's, the young seeker from the Katha Upanishad. Nachiketa was unlike most children. When his father, the sage Vajasravasa, offered worthless gifts in a ritual, Nachiketa questioned him, only to be angrily sent to Yama, the god of death. But instead of fearing his fate, Nachiketa willingly embraced the unknown, waiting three days at Yama's door.

Granted three boons, he first wished for his father's peace and then for sacred knowledge. But his third wish set him apart—he asked Yama to reveal the truth of existence. Yama tried to tempt him with wealth, pleasure, and power, but Nachiketa refused. "All these things are temporary. I seek the eternal." He transcended to being Man-4 in this case.

What should be done? - Awakening the Instinctive Student

Routine-based education keeps students trapped in Man-1, the state of habitual learning, where they absorb information passively, repeating patterns without questioning their relevance. Breaking this cycle requires a shift toward dynamic, project-based learning, where students engage with concepts actively rather than just reading from textbooks. Learning must become an experience, not just an exercise in memorization. Self-reflection should be at the core of education—students must be taught to observe their own habits, question their routines, and recognize when they are operating on autopilot. Interdisciplinary learning plays a crucial role in this transformation, allowing students to connect ideas across subjects rather than viewing knowledge in isolated silos.

When learning becomes fluid, engaging, and self-directed, students break free from mechanical repetition and step into Man-4—conscious, awakened learning.

Gurdjieff's Model in Relation to Education

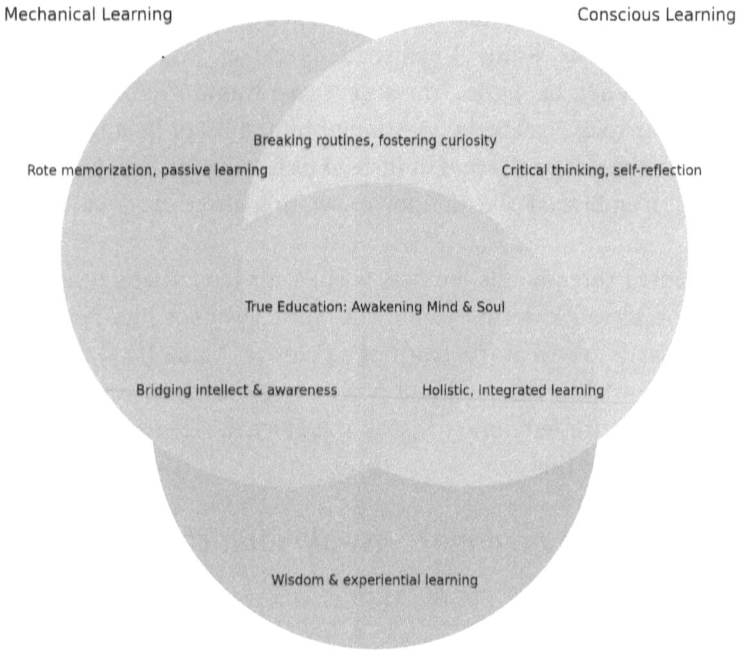

Mapping Education with Gurdjieff's Philosophy

1.3 Bridging Ancient Wisdom and Modern Education: Reviving the Path to True Learning

The gap between ancient wisdom and modern education is not just a philosophical discussion—it is a lived experience, one that affects millions of students around the world. It is the difference between knowing and understanding, between intelligence and wisdom, between memory and self-realization.

If we wish to awaken education from its slumber, we must restore the lost bridge between external learning and inner transformation. Let us explore how we can do this through three powerful approaches: inquiry-based learning, meditation and self-awareness practices, and holistic education.

a) Inquiry-Based Learning – Awakening the Mind Through Questions

Let's take a look at Kabir, a young boy who studies in a top international school in Bangalore. Kabir sat in his classroom, staring blankly at the board. The teacher was explaining Newton's Third Law of Motion:

"For every action, there is an equal and opposite reaction."

Kabir raised his hand hesitantly. *"Ma'am, does this law also apply to human emotions?"*

The class erupted into giggles. The teacher sighed. *"Out of context. Kabir, please focus on physics. We are not discussing philosophy."*

Kabir lowered his hand, his question left unanswered.

This is the modern classroom scenario, where students are trained to absorb information but not to question it. There is no room for curiosity, no space for philosophical reflection. Education has become a rigid structure of correct and incorrect answers, leaving no space for wonder, exploration, or deep thinking.

Now contrast this with a scene from Mahabharata, an epic from ancient India, where Arjun once sat before his mentor, Krishna, filled with doubt and despair. In the middle of the battlefield of Kurukshetra, surrounded by chaos, he asked a question:

"Krishna, what is my duty? Should I fight this war, or should I walk away?"

Instead of dismissing his question, Krishna engaged in a profound dialogue, answering him through the Bhagavad Gita. Arjun's questions were not silenced—they were encouraged, explored, and answered with depth.

This was the essence of ancient learning—not dictating knowledge, but guiding students towards wisdom through inquiry. Instead of suppressing questions, great teachers invited them.

What should be done? - Bringing Inquiry-Based Learning to Modern Classrooms

Education must be redefined as a journey of inquiry, not just a system of answers. Classrooms should not be places where students memorize facts but spaces where they question, reflect, and seek deeper understanding. The role of a teacher is not to dictate knowledge but to inspire curiosity—to encourage students to ask questions that challenge their thinking, not just about their subjects but about their lives. Science, history, and mathematics should not be reduced to formulas and dates; they must be explored as pathways to understanding reality itself. Every lesson should integrate philosophical discussions, allowing students to see beyond textbooks and connect knowledge to their own experiences. A true learning environment is one where curiosity is not punished but rewarded, where open dialogue thrives, and where questioning is seen as a sign of intelligence, not defiance. A classroom that nurtures wonder is a classroom where real education begins.

b) *Meditation and Self-Awareness Practices – Awakening the Heart and Soul*

Imagine a young girl named Aisha, a top student in her school. She is intelligent, ambitious, and hardworking. Yet, beneath her success lies a mind consumed by anxiety and relentless pressure. Every night, she struggles to sleep, her thoughts racing with exam fears, expectations, and an uncertain future. Her teachers praise her achievements, but no one sees the turmoil within. She is excelling, but she is not at peace.

Now, let's go back 2,500 years. Another young woman, Khema, once a queen, had everything—wealth, status, beauty—but like Aisha, she was restless. The fear of imperfection and the uncertainty of life tormented her. When she encountered the Buddha, his words struck something deep within her: *"Everything you cling to is fleeting, but peace lies in seeing things as they are."* Through his guidance, Khema let go of her illusions, embraced wisdom, and found true inner peace. (*Therigatha 2.3*)

What separates Aisha from Khema? One is trapped in constant striving, believing happiness lies in the next achievement, while the other has discovered the stillness within, realizing that true fulfilment is not in external success but in inner balance and awareness.

Modern education teaches students how to think but not how to reflect, how to achieve but not how to be at peace. In the pursuit of excellence, we have forgotten the wisdom of self-awareness, mindfulness, and inner stillness. If we wish to create not just high achievers, but fulfilled human beings, we must restore this lost dimension of education.

What should be done? - Bringing Meditation and Self-Awareness to Modern Schools

Modern education fills students' minds with endless information, yet it leaves them overwhelmed, anxious, and emotionally drained.

Schools push for academic excellence but rarely equip students with the mental clarity and resilience needed to process challenges without breaking under pressure. A mind flooded with stress cannot think critically, retain knowledge effectively, or approach learning with joy. Education must go beyond mere instruction—it must create space for reflection, emotional awareness, and inner balance. Mindfulness practices in schools can transform learning from a passive, pressure-driven exercise into an experience of conscious engagement. When students begin their day with a few moments of silence, they develop the ability to pause, process, and observe their own thoughts without being consumed by them. Encouraging self-awareness over reaction, teaching students to acknowledge their emotions rather than being controlled by them, is just as crucial as academic success. A truly educated mind is not just one that is filled with knowledge—it is one that is clear, steady, and capable of handling life with wisdom and inner peace.

c) Holistic Education – Awakening the Whole Human Being

Ravi is a 17-year-old student with a passion for music and poetry. But his parents want him to become an engineer.

"Music is a hobby," they say. "It won't feed you."

So, Ravi buries his passion and follows the path of logic, numbers, and equations. Years later, he is successful but deeply unfulfilled. He has everything except joy.

Ravi's story is not new; it has reverberated across generations. The struggle between passion and practicality is as old as time, but history offers examples of those who refused to bury their true calling. One such figure is Bharata, the legendary playwright and composer of the Natya Shastra.

He was born into a time when Vedic studies and ritualistic knowledge were considered the primary forms of education. But Bharata's inclination toward drama, music, and storytelling was unconventional. In an era where practical professions like priesthood, administration, or warfare were given importance, Bharata pursued the art of expression, emotions, and human psychology. His passion led him to compile the Natya Shastra, an ancient Sanskrit text that laid the foundation for Indian theatre, dance, and performance arts.

Had Bharata followed the rigid educational norms of his time, he would have remained confined to scriptural recitations and scholarly debates, but his inner calling led him to create an entirely new discipline of knowledge—one that merged intellect with creativity. Today, the Natya Shastra is revered as a timeless guide to the performing arts, proving that education should not suppress creativity but embrace it as a path to deeper understanding.

Bharata's journey speaks for countless students today, like Ravi, who are told to choose "practical" careers over their passions. His story serves as a reminder that true education does not force individuals into predetermined paths—it nurtures their unique talents, allowing them to shape their own destinies, and the goal of education should always be about discovering one's unique path, not forcing them to fit into a mould.

What should be done? - Restoring Holistic Education Today

A truly transformative education system does not measure success by grades, degrees, or standardized achievements alone—it recognizes that intelligence is far more complex, diverse, and multidimensional. Schools must go beyond the narrow definition of academic excellence and acknowledge that creative, emotional, and spiritual intelligence are just as vital as logic and memorization. Every student carries a unique potential that cannot be confined to rigid career paths. Forcing young minds into pre-decided moulds suffocates innovation, originality, and self-discovery. The greatest thinkers, artists, and visionaries did not thrive by following imposed expectations; they thrived because they were allowed to explore, experiment, and evolve. Education must become a space where students can engage with multiple disciplines—where the scientist can be a poet, the musician can be a mathematician, and the philosopher can be an entrepreneur. Knowledge is not meant to be fragmented; it is a vast, interconnected web that must be experienced holistically. Beyond academics, schools must prioritize character development, ethical thinking, and real-life skills, shaping individuals who are not just competent professionals but also compassionate, self-aware, and morally grounded human beings. The purpose of education should never be to simply produce workers for an economy—it must awaken the whole individual, unlocking their potential to contribute meaningfully to the world.

Conclusion: Awakening Education from Its Sleep

Today, education is a vast, mechanized system—producing brilliant minds but disconnected souls.

A student can solve complex equations but cannot handle stress. A student can analyze literature but does not know how to navigate emotions.
A student can pass exams but does not know who they truly are.

We have created a system of learning that is divorced from wisdom, of intelligence that is devoid of self-awareness.

But change is possible.

Imagine a world where students begin their day with silence, centering themselves before diving into knowledge.
Imagine a world where teachers encourage deep questioning, not just correct answers.
Imagine a world where education is not a race, but a journey of self-discovery.

Such a world is not a fantasy—it is a return to the lost wisdom of ancient education. It is an education that awakens rather than numbs, enlightens rather than conditions, liberates rather than imprisons.

For in the end, true education is not about memorizing facts, passing exams, or securing jobs.

It is about awakening the soul, illuminating the mind, and igniting the spirit.

And that, above all else, is the purpose of learning.

EDUCATION AS A PATH TO CONSCIOUS EVOLUTION

Introduction: Why Does Education Need Deliberate Evolution?

Why do we educate? Is it merely to memorize information, pass exams, and secure jobs? Or is it meant to serve a deeper purpose- to awaken something within us?

In today's world, education often remains trapped at the lower levels of human evolution. Most people operate mechanically, driven by survival, emotions, and intellect, without ever stepping into the level of self-awareness, wisdom, or transcendence. G.I. Gurdjieff's model of human evolution (Man-1 to Man-7), as discussed in the previous chapter, presents a powerful framework for understanding how individuals grow- not just intellectually, but spiritually and existentially.

Instead of dwelling in the first 3 levels, Man-1, Man-2, Man-3, we should focus on being Man-4, slowly understanding the further levels, because they represent the higher stages of human evolution. In these levels education truly transforms from mechanical conditioning into a conscious journey of awakening.

Now comes the big question. Why Is This Evolution Necessary?

Breaking Free from Mechanical Existence

Most individuals move through life reactively, shaped by external forces rather than conscious choice. From birth, societal norms, cultural conditioning, and education systems dictate their beliefs, emotions, and aspirations. They wake up, work, consume, and sleep, and they never truly question the 'why' behind their thoughts and actions. Without deliberate effort, they remain in a state of sleep-like existence, functioning at the levels of Man-1 (instinct-driven), Man-2 (emotion-driven), or Man-3 (intellect-driven), as described by Gurdjieff's model of human evolution.

Man-1 operates purely on biological instincts- survival, hunger, and self-preservation. Many students in impoverished conditions struggle at this level, their education secondary to their fight for basic needs. Man-2, on the other hand, is driven by emotions- fear, attachment, and societal approval. A student at this stage may study not out of curiosity but out of the fear of failure or desire for validation. They are caught in cycles of anxiety, pressure, and conditioned emotional responses. Man-3 represents intellect-driven existence- where a person can be highly knowledgeable but still mechanical in thought. This is the student who excels in academics but never questions the system- who memorizes formulas but does not understand the beauty of mathematics, who scores well but remains detached from true learning.

History has shown how dangerous this mechanical existence can be. The Nazi officers who carried out mass atrocities were not uneducated, they were intelligent, well-trained individuals functioning as Man-3. They followed orders without moral reflection or higher awareness. In contrast, those who broke free from this conditioned existence such as Socrates, Buddha, or even

Nachiketa from the Upanishads, transcended societal programming and began their journey toward true wisdom.

Education, at its best, should awaken students from this robotic cycle. It should encourage them to pause, reflect, and engage with their learning rather than merely follow instructions. Without this shift, even the brightest minds will remain asleep, operating within the framework set for them, never realizing their full potential.

The Shift from Knowledge to Wisdom

Memorizing information does not equate to wisdom. A person can store thousands of facts yet remain blind to the deeper truths of existence. This is why education cannot stop at knowledge accumulation; it must evolve into wisdom cultivation.

The distinction between Man-3 (intellect-driven) and Man-4 (conscious learning) lies in awareness and depth of understanding. The intellectual mind processes data, analyzes trends, and solves problems, but it often lacks insight and self-reflection. Many scientists, engineers, and philosophers have been intellectual giants, yet without emotional and spiritual wisdom, their knowledge remained incomplete.

A striking example of this contrast is seen in the Mahabharata. Karna and Arjun were equally skilled warriors, equally trained in divine weapons. Yet, one remained bound by ego and emotion, while the other transcended toward wisdom. Karna, despite his intellect, remained trapped in the emotional conflicts of loyalty and resentment, never questioning whether he was on the right side of dharma. Arjuna, under the guidance of Krishna, broke free from self-doubt and discovered his higher purpose. This transformation from intellectual ability to conscious realization is the journey from Man-3 to Man-4 and beyond.

Modern education fails because it prioritizes knowledge over wisdom. Students are trained to excel in competitive exams but are rarely encouraged to question their beliefs, reflect on their emotions, or explore the ethical implications of their actions. The greatest thinkers in history- Buddha, Socrates, and Swami Vivekananda, did not merely acquire knowledge; they sought wisdom. They questioned the nature of reality, the meaning of existence, and the purpose of human life. If education does not cultivate this deeper inquiry, it remains a hollow pursuit, producing scholars who know much but understand little.

Conscious Evolution is the Purpose of True Education

Education must not be confined to feeding the mind with facts, it must awaken the whole being. A true learning system should engage mind, body, and soul, nurturing not just intelligence but emotional depth, ethical clarity, and spiritual awareness. Yet, modern schools and universities rarely encourage this holistic transformation.

This principle is deeply embedded in India's ancient Gurukul system. A student under a guru was not just taught literature, mathematics, or warfare, they were also trained in self-discipline, meditation, ethics, and self-inquiry. Learning was not limited to memorization; it was an experience of the mind expanding toward higher consciousness. The great figures from our mythology and history, whether it was Krishna, Chanakya, or even Valmiki, they did not simply absorb information; they transformed themselves.

Now let's contrast this with the colonial model of education that persists today. Designed to create obedient workers rather than awakened thinkers, the modern system prioritizes industrial efficiency over intellectual liberation. Schools produce employees for the workforce, not seekers of truth. The British education model, as implemented in India, was never meant to create leaders; it was designed to create clerks and bureaucrats. This approach still lingers, and students are trained to follow, not to question.

But conscious evolution is not optional. Humanity must break away from passive learning and move toward active self-discovery. If education continues to exist as a system of job preparation rather than soul awakening, society will continue producing individuals who are intelligent but spiritually and emotionally hollow. The Gita's wisdom, the Upanishads' inquiry, and even modern neuroscience confirm that human potential expands only when knowledge is integrated with inner awareness.

True education is a journey of awakening, not just a path to employment. It must guide students beyond rote learning, beyond exams, beyond academic competition, and lead them toward self-awareness, clarity, and mastery over their own minds. A civilization thrives not when its people are merely educated but when they are truly awake.

The Journey Toward Higher Education

Gurdjieff's Man-4 to Man-7 stages offer a vision of education that moves beyond mechanical learning, guiding students toward self-realization, mastery, and transcendence. To understand this concept of evolution better, let us turn to one of the most profound spiritual stories in Indian tradition- the story of Nachiketa from the Katha Upanishad.

The Story of Nachiketa: A Boy Who Chose Wisdom Over Everything Else

This ancient tale is all about a Father's Sacrifice and a Boy's Question. Let's read this:

We are looking back at a time when rituals and offerings to the gods were considered the key to spiritual success. There lived a great sage named Vajashravas who sought to gain divine favor. He decided to perform a grand yajna (sacrifice), giving away cows to Brahmins. However, the cows he chose were old, weak, and barren, unfit for any real use.

His young son, Nachiketa, watched this with doubt and curiosity. He was a child with deep introspection and had a truth-seeking mindset, he invariably questioned his father:

"Father, to whom will you give me away?"

At first, his father ignored him. But Nachiketa kept repeating his question. Frustrated by his persistence, as most Indian parent would be, Vajashravas angrily declared:

"I give you to Yama—the Lord of Death!"

Obedient and fearless, Nachiketa took his father's words seriously. He walked alone in pursuit to seek an audience with Yama, and at the gate of Yamloka he waited patiently for three days as Yama was not home.

Upon Yama's return, he was moved by the boy's dedication and offered him three boons (wishes). Nachiketa's first two wishes were simple and selfless, but the third was profound:

"Tell me, O Lord of Death, what happens after we die? What is the truth of existence?"

Yama hesitated as this was the greatest of all secrets. He tried to distract Nachiketa, offering him kingdoms, wealth, and power; a long and pleasurable life; and Celestial enjoyments beyond imagination.

But Nachiketa remained firm:

"O Death, these pleasures fade like a dream. I seek only truth. Teach me the secret of the Self."

Gurdjieff's path from Man-1 to Man-7 is a journey of deliberate evolution, and Nachiketa's story from the Katha Upanishad is a perfect illustration of this transformation. Initially, he encounters the world through Man-1, Man-2, and Man-3, rejecting material distractions, questioning the rituals performed by his father, and refusing to be swayed by temporary pleasures. His rejection of wealth, comfort, and superficial rewards signifies his shift beyond instinct (Man-1), emotions (Man-2), and intellectual reasoning alone (Man-3). Instead, he steps onto the path of Man-4, where learning becomes a process of self-integration rather than mere information absorption. His encounter with Yama, the god of death, is a test of his resolve, and through deep self-awareness and unshakable determination, he moves toward Man-5, embodying persistence and the courage to seek the highest truth. As he persists despite all distractions and obstacles, he enters the final stages of Man-6 and Man-7, where he receives direct knowledge of the Atman—the eternal Self—and reaches ultimate enlightenment. His journey is not one of passive acceptance but of conscious transformation, proving that a true learner does not settle for superficial knowledge but instead seeks mastery of the Self, the highest purpose of education.

Maslow's Hierarchy and Gurdjieff's Model: The Psychology of Conscious Learning

"Education is not about filling the mind with facts, but about awakening the soul to its fullest potential."

Deeper Psychological Structure of Learning

Let's explore how Maslow's hierarchy of needs and Gurdjieff's model align in the journey of two students, Ramesh and Meera, whose paths in education unfurl in different ways.

Ramesh is an exceptionally bright student, the kind every teacher praise and every parent boasts about. He memorizes textbooks with ease, scores top marks in every exam, and follows the system with perfect discipline. Yet, beneath this veneer of success, he is constantly anxious, burdened by expectations, and terrified of failure. His education is built on survival and security—he studies not out of love for learning, but out of fear of falling behind. Grades define his worth; approval shapes his identity. Like a machine programmed for efficiency, he excels in rote learning but never pauses to question, never asks himself why he is learning in the first place. Despite achieving academic success, he remains unfulfilled—trapped in the lower levels of Maslow's hierarchy and bound to the early stages of Gurdjieff's model (Man-1 to Man-3).

Meera, on the other hand, approaches education differently. She is equally intelligent, yet unlike Ramesh, she is not content with simply knowing—she wants to understand. She questions the rules, challenges the curriculum, and seeks wisdom beyond what the textbooks offer. For her, learning is not about external rewards; it is about self-discovery. While others obsess over exams, she looks for meaning in what she studies, finding connections between subjects, applying knowledge to life, and using reflection as a tool for growth. Meera is moving beyond external validation—she is ascending from intellectual accumulation (Man-3) to conscious awareness (Man-4 and beyond).

Their futures are shaped by their approach to learning, and needless to say, will be dramatically different. Ramesh may continue to achieve, but without self-awareness, he will always chase success without ever feeling truly fulfilled. Meera, however, will grow not just in knowledge but in wisdom, transforming herself through learning rather than being controlled by it. Her education is not just about facts—it is about awakening. We all remember Rancho and Chatur from the movie 3 idiots, don't we?

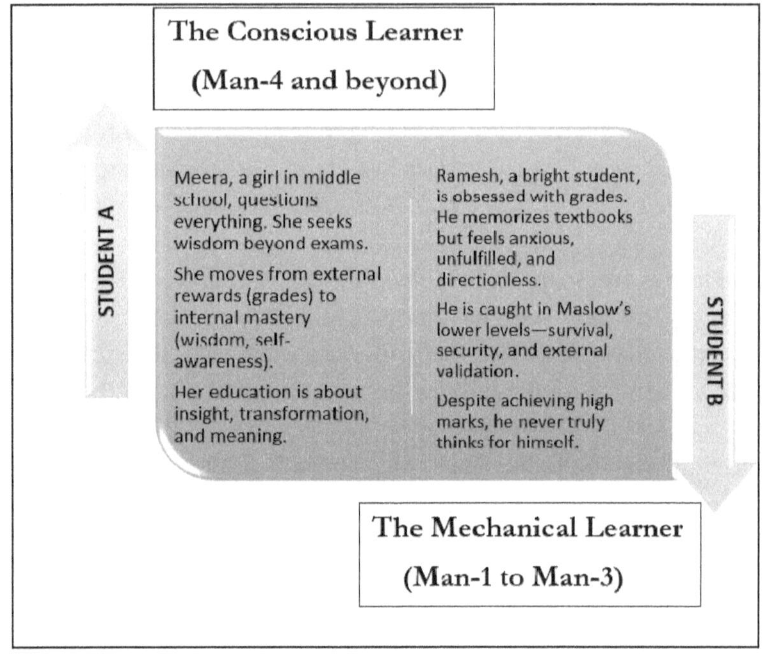

Pic: Case study: Meera and Ramesh's journey

Education is more than just the transmission of knowledge; it is the pathway from mechanical existence to conscious evolution. When viewed through the lens of Maslow's hierarchy of needs and Gurdjieff's stages of human development, education emerges as the bridge between instinctual survival and higher self-awareness.

At the most fundamental level, students exist in Man-1, driven by instinct and survival. Their primary concern is security—physical, emotional, and psychological. A child who feels unsafe, either at home or in school, cannot engage in higher learning. Education's first duty is to create an environment where students feel secure, supported, and valued so that learning is not a battle for survival but a journey of exploration.

As students move forward, they enter Man-2 and Man-3, the areas of emotional conditioning and intellect. Here, the need for belonging, self-esteem, and social validation takes center stage. Many students become trapped at this level, chasing grades, external recognition, and approval from teachers and parents. True education must do more than teach information, it must develop emotional resilience, critical thinking, and self-awareness. Without this, students remain reactive, conforming to societal expectations rather than questioning their own beliefs and purpose.

For those who break free from the cycle of external validation, the shift into Man-4 and Man-5 begins, the stage of self-actualization. This is where students no longer learn just to achieve but to understand, integrate, and grow. Education at this level should encourage self-inquiry, helping students connect knowledge with deeper meaning, guiding them to see learning as a transformative force rather than a mechanical process.

At the highest stages, Man-6 and Man-7, learning becomes wisdom. Here, education must transcend textbooks and exams, inspiring students to seek truth, purpose, and inner mastery. Knowledge is no longer an external pursuit but an internal awakening. The rare individuals who reach this stage, the true seekers, the enlightened minds, the awakened souls, become the ones who shape history and redefine the world.

Education's role, then, is not merely to fill minds with facts but to awaken the whole being. It must guide students from survival to self-awareness, from intellect to insight, from knowledge to wisdom. This is the true purpose of learning, not just to train minds but to liberate them.

Education's Role in Moving from Mechanical to Conscious Learning

Maslow's Needs	Gurdjieff's Stages	Education's Role
Survival (food, security)	Man-1 (Instinct)	Ensure students feel safe and supported.
Belonging & Esteem	Man-2 & Man-3 (Emotion & Intellect)	Teach emotional resilience and critical thinking.
Self-Actualization	Man-4 & Man-5 (Awakening)	Guide students toward self-awareness and purpose.
Self-Transcendence	Man-6 & Man-7 (Mastery)	Inspire deep wisdom and true enlightenment.

Pic: Maslow's Needs mapped with Gurdjieff's Stages

Awakening Education from Its Sleep

Education is not just about training the mind but about awakening the soul. We must move beyond mechanical learning and create schools, universities, and societies that nurture Man-4 to Man-7 thinking.

"A true education does not create workers. It creates thinkers, visionaries, and awakened souls."

Will we continue teaching students how to memorize, or will we teach them how to truly live?

Bloom's Taxonomy – The way to Conscious Education

Why Do Some Students Awaken, While Others Remain Asleep?

Imagine two students in the same classroom. One is deeply engaged, questioning ideas, connecting theories, and finding meaning. The other is mechanically memorizing, preparing for an exam, but without any deep understanding or curiosity.

What causes this difference?

The answer lies in how education is structured. Modern education often remains at lower levels of thinking, i.e. focusing on rote learning, repetition, and surface-level understanding. However, true education should elevate learners to higher consciousness, helping them engage with knowledge in a way that transforms their mind and being.

To understand this, let's explore Bloom's Taxonomy, a six-level hierarchy of cognitive development, and see how it aligns with Indian philosophies of knowledge and self-realization.

Bloom's Taxonomy as a Spiritual Journey

Bloom's Taxonomy was developed by Benjamin Bloom in 1956 as a framework to define different levels of learning. What many don't realize is that it closely mirrors ancient Indian learning systems, which describe knowledge as a progressive journey from ignorance to self-mastery.

To make this concept clearer, let's imagine a story of a young seeker named Ajata, who embarks on a journey toward wisdom.

Ajata's Journey Through the Six Stages of Learning

1. Remembering: The First Steps of a Seeker

Ajata is a curious student; he approaches a wise guru in the Himalayas. His first task is to memorize sacred verses, philosophical texts, and historical lessons.

At this stage, learning is passive, much like how students today memorize formulas, facts, and definitions without necessarily understanding them. The knowledge remains on the surface, untested by reflection or inquiry.

2. Understanding: Asking Questions

One day, Ajata asks his guru, *"Guruji, I have memorized many scriptures, but I do not understand their meaning. Why did Lord Krishna speak of detachment in the Bhagavad Gita? What does it truly mean?"* The guru smiles, for now, Ajata is beginning to understand. He no longer just remembers words but questions and seeks meaning. This is the stage where students grasp concepts instead of just reciting them.

In modern education, this is where teachers should focus on discussion and comprehension rather than just syllabus completion, ensuring that learning becomes an active process of inquiry.

3. Applying: Turning Knowledge Into Action

One day, Ajata sees a poor traveller struggling to cross a river. He recalls a lesson from his guru about selfless service and decides to help the traveller. His guru watches and says, *"Now, you are no longer just a student of words. You are a student of action."* This stage is about applying knowledge to real-life situations, making learning meaningful beyond the classroom.

In schools, students should be encouraged to use what they learn—whether through experiments, projects, or real-world applications that bridge theory and practice.

4. Analyzing: Seeing the Bigger Picture

Ajata begins connecting different teachings and asks, *"Guruji, I see that the idea of Dharma appears in the Vedas, the Upanishads, and the Bhagavad Gita, but each describes it differently. What is the real meaning of Dharma?"* Now, he is analyzing—breaking down complex ideas, comparing different viewpoints, and forming deeper insights.

In education, this is the stage where students should compare theories, critique arguments, and explore different perspectives. Unfortunately, modern education often skips this stage because it is easier to test memory than to assess analytical thinking.

5. Evaluating: Independent Thought and Judgment

Ajata now questions even his guru. He debates, challenges ideas, and seeks his own interpretations. His guru tells him, *"You are ready, Ajata. True wisdom is not in blindly accepting knowledge, but in forming your own understanding."* This stage is about critical thinking, evaluating ideas, and forming personal judgments.

In education, students at this level should engage in research, debate, and critical discussions, questioning societal norms and the very structures of knowledge they have been given.

6. Creating: The Birth of a Master

One day, Ajata becomes the guru himself. He develops his own teachings, adding to the wisdom of the past. He has reached the highest stage, creation. This is when students generate new knowledge, become innovators, and contribute to society.

Sadly, most modern education never reaches this stage, it stops at remembering and understanding, never empowering students to think beyond what has already been taught, to create, and to transform knowledge into something new.

Indian Philosophies That Align With Bloom's Taxonomy

The principles of Indian philosophy resonate deeply with Bloom's Taxonomy, which outlines the stages of cognitive development from basic recall to higher-order thinking and creation (Bloom, 1956). While modern education has largely been structured around memorization and standardization, ancient Indian wisdom emphasizes experiential learning, self-inquiry, and conscious evolution. Among the many philosophical traditions, Jnana Yoga, Karma Yoga, and Vedantic philosophy align closely with Bloom's cognitive framework.

Jnana Yoga, or the Path of Knowledge, is the intellectual and philosophical pursuit of truth. Rooted in the Upanishads, this discipline involves moving from mere information toward deep understanding and realization (Vivekananda, 1896). In Bloom's Taxonomy, the lower stages, remembering and understanding, correspond to the early phases of Jnana Yoga, where a student engages with scriptures, listens to discourses, and absorbs knowledge. However, Jnana Yoga does not stop at information, it demands analysis, reflection, and evaluation, much like Bloom's higher-order thinking. A seeker must engage in self-inquiry (Vichara) and break down illusions to distinguish between relative and absolute truth. Just as evaluation in Bloom's model requires forming judgments based on criteria and evidence, Jnana Yoga demands that a seeker challenge conventional knowledge and arrive at wisdom through deep questioning and reasoning.

Karma Yoga, the Path of Action, is closely aligned with application in Bloom's Taxonomy. Rooted in the Bhagavad Gita, Karma Yoga emphasizes putting knowledge into practice through selfless action. While Jnana Yoga emphasizes wisdom through contemplation, Karma Yoga insists that true understanding manifests only when applied in real life (Easwaran, 1985). In Bloom's model, a student at the application stage must go beyond theoretical learning and demonstrate understanding through practice. A student of Karma Yoga does not merely study concepts like dharma (duty) and selfless service but actively embodies these principles in daily actions. This corresponds with education that prioritizes experiential learning, projects, and real-world application over rote memorization.

Vedantic philosophy aligns with the progressive movement from lower (mechanical) knowledge to higher (experiential) wisdom. The Mundaka Upanishad (1.1.5) distinguishes between Parā Vidyā (higher knowledge, self-realization) and Aparā Vidyā (lower knowledge, intellectual learning). Aparā Vidyā represents the initial levels of Bloom's taxonomy, remembering and understanding, where knowledge remains external and mechanical. However, true education, according to Vedanta, is not about accumulating facts but about realizing the deeper truths through direct experience (Anubhava). This coincides with Bloom's highest level, creation, where knowledge is not just absorbed but transformed and innovated upon. Swami Vivekananda (1893) argued that education should not merely provide information but inspire self-discovery and realization, aligning closely with Vedantic teachings on the journey from intellectual learning to direct experiential wisdom.

It can be argued that our Indian philosophy and Bloom's Taxonomy share a common vision of progressive learning, where knowledge is not an end but a means to deeper understanding, practical application, and ultimately, self-realization. As modern education increasingly relies on standardized testing and artificial intelligence, the wisdom of these ancient traditions reminds us that true learning must move beyond information toward wisdom, action, and inner transformation.

Modern Education and the Crisis of Unawakened Learning

Despite decades of research on learning, psychology, and pedagogy, a deep crisis lingers in modern education. Students across the world, from elite institutions to underfunded schools, increasingly feel disengaged, uninspired, and disconnected from the learning process. The paradox is striking. While education systems have grown more sophisticated, student curiosity and intrinsic motivation have steadily declined. The root of the problem lies in the fact that education remains stuck in the lower stages of Bloom's taxonomy, focusing on memorization and repetition rather than deep understanding, analysis, and creation.

One of the most glaring examples of unawakened learning is the dominance of rote-learning factories. In India and many parts of the world, students preparing for high-stakes exams like NEET, JEE, and UPSC spend years memorizing vast amounts of information without ever grasping the underlying concepts. Their success is measured by their ability to regurgitate facts under time constraints, rather than their ability to apply, evaluate, or innovate. This kind of education does not create thinkers, problem-solvers, or visionaries, it produces human calculators trained for exams rather than for life. But the question of the hour is, with the rise of AI and its ability to process unimaginable amount of information, how relevant would rote memorisation-based exams be in a long run?

We also should note that the failure of application-based learning further highlights this crisis. Countless engineering graduates complete their degrees without gaining any practical, hands-on experience in their field. Despite earning qualifications, they enter the workforce unprepared for real-world challenges because their education emphasized theory over practice. The result is an education-to-employment mismatch, where students have degrees but lack the skills employers seek. This disconnect between academic learning and practical competence exposes the fundamental flaw in an education system that prioritizes grades over mastery, completion over comprehension.

Beyond this, there is a widespread lack of creativity and critical thinking in schools and universities as well. Instead of fostering an environment where students are encouraged to question, analyze, and explore, traditional education systems reward those who simply repeat what textbooks say. Original thought is rarely valued; compliance is. A student who memorizes a pre-approved definition receives high marks, while a student who challenges conventional wisdom is often seen as disruptive. This suppression of intellectual curiosity and independent thought results in generations of students who know how to follow instructions but not how to create, critique, or innovate.

Fixing this crisis requires a radical shift in the way we approach learning. Education must move beyond textbook-driven instruction and embrace projects, discussions, and creative exploration. Students should engage in hands-on learning experiences where knowledge is applied in meaningful ways, bridging the gap between theory and practice. Schools must encourage debate, critical analysis, and interdisciplinary learning, allowing students to connect knowledge across different subjects rather than confining them to rigid academic silos. Most importantly, education must shift from a grade-oriented evaluation system to a mastery-based approach, where students grow at their own pace, developing deep understanding rather than simply meeting deadlines. Although some schools and colleges in India are awakening to the concepts of Project based learning and Experiential learning, but that would probably be just 1% of the entire lot.

The crisis of unawakened learning is not just about education, it is about the future of humanity. If students continue to be trained as passive absorbers of information rather than active creators of knowledge, society will stagnate. To reclaim wisdom and transform education, we must move beyond teaching for exams and begin teaching for life.

The Einstein-Tagore Conversation: A Meeting of Science and Spirituality

It was July 14, 1930, in Berlin - a time when science was unraveling the deepest mysteries of the universe, and philosophy was grappling with the shifting nature of truth (Dutta & Robinson,

1995). Albert Einstein, the man from the West whose equations had redefined time and space, sat across from Rabindranath Tagore, the poet-philosopher from the East whose words had stirred the human soul. Their meeting was not one of pleasantries; it was a collision of two ways of thinking—scientific materialism and spiritual humanism (Einstein & Tagore, 1930).

Einstein was deeply rooted in the world of physics and objective reality. He was eager to engage in philosophical discourse. Tagore, who embodied centuries of Indian wisdom, welcomed the conversation. And soon, they found themselves drawn to a question that has haunted thinkers across civilizations:

What is truth?

Einstein posed the question in his usual direct manner:

"Do you believe in the independent existence of reality?" (Holton, 1971).

It was a question that had long weighed the Western scientific thought, that had long believed in an objective universe, the kind that existed with or without human perception. For Newton, the world was deterministic, governed by absolute laws. For Einstein, it was relativistic, but still bound by universal principles. In both cases, reality was something external, out there, independent of human experience (Holton, 1971).

Tagore, however, had a different perspective shaped by Vedantic philosophy. He reasoned that reality is not separate from consciousness (Dutta & Robinson, 1995). With his usual quiet confidence, he replied:

"The world is a human world. Truth is not independent of the human mind." (Einstein & Tagore, 1930).

To Einstein, this was unsettling. Science, after all, sought universal laws, truths that remained unchanged whether or not humans were there to perceive them. Gravity would still function, planets would still move, and relativity would still hold, even if there were no one to observe them (Holton, 1971).

But Tagore was not denying reality itself, rather, he was challenging the assumption that truth exists in isolation from human experience. He explained that science, art, and philosophy are all bound to perception. A melody is not just a sequence of vibrations; it exists in the listener's mind. A painting is not just color on canvas; it is an emotional resonance within the observer (Dutta & Robinson, 1995).

Einstein listened intently. He was not one to dismiss ideas outright, after all, he had spent his life breaking paradigms, challenging Newton's certainties, and redefining what humanity thought it knew about the universe. And now, sitting across from him was a mind that questioned something even deeper, not just the laws of physics, but the very nature of how we understand reality (Holton, 1971).

Was truth an absolute, existing beyond human interpretation? Or was it, as Tagore suggested, something inherently shaped by consciousness?

The conversation did not reach a conclusion, how could it? The debate between objective reality and subjective perception has continued for centuries and will likely persist for many more. But their exchange left an imprint on both men. Einstein respected the poetic depth of Tagore's thought, and Tagore admired the precision of Einstein's reasoning (Einstein & Tagore, 1930).

Perhaps, in that moment, they both glimpsed a deeper truth, that science and spirituality are not opposites, but complementary forces searching for the same ultimate understanding.

The Essence of This Conversation in Education

The conversation between Einstein and Tagore is more than an intellectual dialogue, it is a lesson for education itself (Dutta & Robinson, 1995).

If learning focuses only on facts and data, it becomes mechanistic, stripped of meaning. If it focuses only on emotions and interpretation, it risks becoming unstructured, lacking discipline. A truly awakened education must balance both: the precision of science with the depth of human experience (Holton,

1971).

As Educators, when we design modern curricula and prepare students for an uncertain future, we must ask ourselves:

Are we teaching objective knowledge without its subjective meaning?

Are we training the mind while neglecting the soul?

Tagore's wisdom reminds us that knowledge is not just about what exists, but how we experience, interpret, and shape it (Einstein & Tagore, 1930). Whereas, Einstein's legacy teaches us that truth-seeking requires deep inquiry and constant questioning (Holton, 1971).

And this deepens the idea that the true purpose of learning can never be merely to know, but to awaken.

Pic: Albert Einstein (Left) and Rabindranath Tagore (right)

The Future of Conscious Learning: Awakening Education from Its Sleep

As the world accelerates toward an era of artificial intelligence, hyper-connectivity, and knowledge at our fingertips, one question remains: What is the future of education if it does not awaken consciousness?

For centuries, education has been a means of survival, producing thinkers, workers, scientists, and leaders who have built civilizations. But as Gurdjieff warned, most of humanity operates in a state of sleep, moving through life reactively, without self-awareness. If our education system does not change, it will continue to produce the same unconscious minds, only armed with more information but no greater wisdom.

The Indian Upanishads, the wisdom of Tagore and Vivekananda, and even modern thinkers like Jiddu Krishnamurti remind us that education is not meant to be a mere transfer of knowledge, it is meant to be a transformation of being.

But what does a conscious education look like? What happens when learning moves beyond the mechanical and into the realm of awakening?

1. The Shift from Knowledge to Wisdom

Education today is obsessed with knowledge acquisition: grades, degrees, test scores. But what if schools and universities focused instead on wisdom cultivation?

A child learning science should not just memorize Newton's laws but also ask: *What does gravity teach us about the nature of the universe and our place in it?*

A student studying literature should not just analyze themes but also wonder: *How does this story mirror my own journey toward self-awareness?*

A future leader should not just study economics and policy but also question: *How do my decisions shape the consciousness of the people I serve?*

When education shifts from being a mere deposit of facts to a living dialogue with truth, we no longer just create professionals, we create awakened human beings.

2. Technology and the Danger of Mechanized Learning

With AI and machine learning advancing rapidly, we stand on the edge of a paradox. Never before has knowledge been so accessible, yet never before has learning been so shallow.

If AI can answer any question in seconds, does that mean we have become more intelligent?

If students can pass exams by using ChatGPT, does that mean they have learned?

If every piece of information is at our fingertips, does that mean we understand it?

Gurdjieff's Man-1, Man-2, Man-3 reminds us that education without inner work only strengthens our mechanical nature - we react, but we do not think; we remember, but we do not understand; we accumulate, but we do not awaken.

A future of conscious learning will require that we balance technological advancement with deep, intentional education, a system where AI is not just a tool for efficiency but a mirror for reflection. Instead of making students passive consumers of information, technology must help them see their own blind spots, biases, and unconscious patterns.

The real danger is not that AI will replace teachers, but that it will replace the need for thinking. The only way forward is to teach students how to engage with knowledge consciously: question it, challenge it, and integrate it into their lives.

3. The Return to Inner Education

What if the schools of the future taught students to observe their own minds as much as they observe the external world?

What if education was not just about reading books but about reading oneself?

Imagine a world where: Meditation is as important as mathematics. Philosophy is as valued as physics. Emotional intelligence is tested as rigorously as analytical intelligence. Self-awareness is considered a subject, not just a personal journey.

This is not utopia; it is a return to the oldest traditions of education. The great Gurukuls of India did not just teach scriptures and sciences, they cultivated character, self-discipline, and higher consciousness. The greatest teachers, from Socrates to the Buddha, did not just give answers, they taught students how to ask the right questions.

If we do not return to inner education, the external world will continue to advance while the human spirit remains asleep. We will build smarter machines but not wiser minds.

4. What Next? The Awakening of Education

The education system today is like a person in deep sleep, dreaming of knowledge but never waking up to its real meaning. The future demands an awakening, a system that does not just fill minds but lights the fire of awareness.

The real question is: Who will lead this change?

Will schools and universities recognize this need?

Will teachers take the risk of teaching for transformation instead of just examination?

Will students demand more than just degrees and jobs, but a deeper understanding of life itself?

Gurdjieff warned that most people will never wake up unless they make a conscious effort. The same is true for education. If we wait for change, it will never come. If we demand it, it will begin.

So, the final question is not whether education will awaken, it is whether we will awaken within it.

And in the end, perhaps the greatest lesson of conscious education is this:

"No teacher can give you wisdom. No school can give you awareness. No book can give you awakening. You must seek it yourself."

The future of learning begins the moment we stop memorizing and start questioning.

So, the question is, *Are you awake?*

CHAPTER THREE

MASLOW'S HIERARCHY OF NEEDS: A PSYCHOLOGICAL FRAMEWORK FOR GROWTH IN EDUCATION

The Forgotten Purpose of Education

Once, there lived a young man, let's call him Rohan. He was a student like millions around the world. From the time he was a child, he was told:

"Study hard, secure a job, and you will be happy."

His parents believed it. His teachers reinforced it. Society rewarded it.

But deep inside, Rohan felt an emptiness he could not name. He had everything: good grades, career prospects, financial stability, and yet something was missing. He did not study out of love for knowledge. He did not work out of passion. He was following a script that had been written for him. One day, by happenstance, he crossed paths with a guru, and he told him:

"You are climbing a ladder. But are you sure it is leaning against the right wall?"

This question haunted Rohan. He had been climbing, but toward what?

This is the story of millions today - students, professionals, and even educators trapped in a system that focuses on survival and success but forgets wisdom and fulfilment.

Abraham Maslow's Hierarchy of Needs gives us a powerful way to understand this struggle. It shows that education is not just about academic success, it is a journey of human evolution.

Like Gurdjieff's Man-1 to Man-7 model, Maslow's theory reveals that most individuals, and most education systems, remain trapped in lower stages of development. Few ever reach self-actualization, let alone transcendence.

But what if education could become a path of awakening, guiding students beyond survival into wisdom, mastery, and enlightenment?

I. *The First Level – Physiological Needs: The Struggle to Learn*

In order to understand this concept better let's look at the story of *The Hungry Student.*

Centuries ago, in a small village called Vaishali, there lived a boy named Kumar. His father was a farmer, and they barely had enough to eat. Every morning, Kumar would walk miles to school in empty stomach and a weak body. When his teacher asked him to recite a lesson, he struggled to concentrate. His hunger was louder than his thoughts. One day, his teacher brought him food and said:

"Kumar, before wisdom comes nourishment. A hungry mind cannot think, and a tired body cannot grow."

Kumar ate, and for the first time, he listened, not just heard, but truly listened.

The Reality Today

Across the world, in and outside classrooms, millions of children struggle with basic needs. For them, education is not just about textbooks and exams, it is a battle against hunger, exhaustion, and poor health. Nutrition, sleep, and overall well-being play a crucial role in cognitive function, yet these fundamental aspects of life are often overlooked in traditional education systems. A child who comes to school on an empty stomach cannot focus, no matter how intelligent they are. A student battling malnutrition, sleep deprivation, or emotional distress will never reach their full learning potential. Before education can elevate the mind, it must first nourish the body.

Philosophical behind this

The wisdom of the Taittiriya Upanishad speaks directly to this reality. It describes the lowest level of human existence as "Annamaya Kosha", the food sheath, where survival dominates all thought. At this stage, the mind is consumed by the most primal needs: food, shelter, and physical security. A student struggling at this level cannot engage in higher learning, just as a seed cannot grow in barren soil. Education's first responsibility, then, is not just to impart knowledge but to create an environment where students are physically and emotionally capable of learning. Schools must recognize that before students can think about academic success, they must be given the foundation of safety, nourishment, and care.

Education's Role in Meeting Basic Needs

Practical initiatives have shown how addressing basic needs can transform education. India's Mid-Day Meal Scheme, which feeds over 120 million children, is one of the largest school meal programs in the world. By ensuring that students receive at least one nutritious meal a day, schools are not just fighting hunger but unlocking the doors to higher learning. Similarly, initiatives that focus on mental and physical well-being, such as providing access to counselors, incorporating mindfulness practices, and prioritizing sleep hygiene are essential in helping students thrive. Health, sleep, and nutrition must be an integral part of the curriculum, not just an afterthought.

A child stuck in Maslow's first stage of survival will never move forward. Like Kumar, only when a child is fed and his basic physiological needs are met, would be able to engage, participate, and learn. Education is not just about feeding the mind, it is about nurturing the whole human being, ensuring that every child has the opportunity to rise beyond survival and reach their full potential.

II. The Second Level – Safety Needs: Fear-Driven Education

Let us now look at the story of *The Student Who Feared Failure*.

Many years ago, in a monastery in Nalanda, a boy named Jayan studied Buddhist philosophy. He was brilliant, but he lived in fear, fear of failing his teacher's expectations, fear of dishonouring his family, fear of punishment. Each morning, he recited scriptures perfectly, but deep inside, he never questioned them. He was afraid that if he asked too much, he would be seen as disrespectful. One day, a wandering monk asked him:

"Jayan, do you study to learn, or do you study to avoid punishment?"

Jayan was shaken. He had never considered this before. For the first time, he asked himself what he truly wanted to know.

The Reality Today

For many students, education is not a journey of discovery, it is a system of fear. Fear of failure, fear of grades, fear of judgment, and fear of disappointing others weigh heavily on young minds. Instead of studying for the love of learning, they study to escape consequences. The joy of exploration is replaced by the anxiety of performance, and in this process, true education is lost. A child who memorizes answers out of fear may pass an exam, but they will never develop a deep understanding of what they have learned. Stress-driven learning may produce short-term results, but it weakens retention, kills creativity, and conditions students to seek validation rather than knowledge. When fear controls learning, education becomes a burden rather than a liberation.

The Bhagavad Gita offers profound insight into this dilemma: *"A man who acts out of fear or desire is bound. A man who acts with wisdom is free."* The essence of true education is not to instil fear but to cultivate wisdom. A system that forces students to comply through pressure and consequences may produce obedient workers, but it will never create thinkers, seekers, or innovators. Education should be a pathway to freedom, helping students break free from the shackles of fear, doubt, and external validation. When students learn not because they must, but because they want to, they enter a space where true understanding and intellectual growth flourish.

Transforming Fear-Based Learning

For education to liberate rather than imprison, it must shift from a punishment-driven system to a curiosity-driven experience. Classrooms should not be spaces where mistakes are punished but where questions are encouraged. When a student hesitates to ask a question out of fear of being judged, learning has already failed. Educators must create safe spaces where intellectual exploration is welcomed, where curiosity is nurtured, and where students are empowered to think, challenge, and grow.

Imagine a classroom where students are not afraid of getting the wrong answer but are excited to discover the right one. Imagine a school where grades do not define self-worth, where learning is an adventure rather than a competition. This is not an idealistic dream; it is a necessity. Education must evolve beyond outdated systems of pressure and fear to become what it was always meant to be, a journey toward wisdom, understanding, and true freedom.

Jayan, once free from fear, truly began his education.

III. The Third Level – Love and Belonging: The Search for Acceptance

Now comes the story of *The Boy Who Wanted to Belong.*

Ravi was a young man in modern-day who resides, let's say, in Mumbai. He worked tirelessly to get into a prestigious engineering college. He believed that success would bring him acceptance and validation.

But once he got there, he realized that his classmates were just as competitive as him. Everyone was too busy proving themselves to connect deeply. And, despite his achievements, he still felt alone. One night, Ravi met an old professor (a guru) who told him:

"Success is meaningless if it is not shared. A true education is not just about knowledge—it is about human connection."

The Reality Today

For many students, education is not a journey of learning but a relentless race—one where grades define self-worth and competition overshadows curiosity. The pressure to outperform peers often turns classrooms into battlegrounds of ranking and comparison, rather than spaces for growth and exploration. In this environment, students measure their value not by what they understand but by how they compare to others.

Yet, human beings are not designed to thrive in isolation. Belonging is a fundamental human need, and learning is most powerful when it is collaborative, not combative. Social belonging—feeling connected to peers, teachers, and the learning process itself—is one of the strongest motivators in education. And yet, most schools focus exclusively on academic achievement while neglecting the deep emotional intelligence that allows students to navigate relationships, build confidence, and find meaning in their learning experiences.

The Upanishads state: *"The greatest knowledge is not of books, but of the self and others."* Education is not just about mastering subjects—it is about understanding oneself and forming meaningful connections with others. A child may excel in math or science, but without empathy, communication, and self-awareness, their education remains incomplete. Knowledge, in its truest form, is not a personal possession but something that flourishes through shared experiences and human relationships.

Schools must recognize that intellectual success alone does not lead to fulfilment. True education must cultivate wisdom, compassion, and emotional resilience, qualities that cannot be measured by grades but are essential for success in life. When students are encouraged to see each other as allies rather than rivals, they develop a deeper sense of purpose, confidence, and belonging.

Creating a Sense of Belonging in Education

In order to transform education into a space of genuine connection, classrooms must shift from competition-driven models to collaborative learning experiences. Instead of ranking students against one another, schools must foster teamwork, peer discussions, and shared problem-solving. Emotional intelligence must be valued as highly as academic achievement, with schools actively teaching skills like self-awareness, empathy, and emotional regulation.

Mentorship programs can also play a crucial role in creating a supportive learning community. When students guide and uplift one another, education ceases to be a lonely struggle and becomes a collaborative journey. Ravi, a student once obsessed with outperforming his peers, came to a realization—education is not just about excelling; it is about connecting. In the end, the true measure of learning is not how much one knows, but how deeply one understands—both the world and the people within it.

Ravi realized that education is not just about excelling, but about connecting.

IV. The Fourth Level – Esteem Needs: The Illusion of Success

Let's look at this story of *The Scholar Who Questioned Success*

In ancient Athens, among the eager disciples of Socrates, there was a young man named Glaucus, whose sharp intellect made him stand out. He was admired for his ability to debate, outwit, and impress, a scholar whose name carried weight in every discussion. Whenever he spoke, people listened. Whenever he argued, he won. His reputation grew, and so did his confidence. He believed he was on the path to true wisdom.

But Socrates saw through him. He observed how Glaucus measured his worth not by the depth of his understanding but by the applause of his audience. One day, after yet another flawless argument, Socrates looked at him and asked, "Glaucus, do you seek wisdom, or do you seek applause?"

For the first time, Glaucus had no answer. He had spent his life chasing approval, validation, and recognition, but had he ever truly sought knowledge for its own sake? In that moment, the illusion of success began to crumble.

The Reality Today

Glaucus' story is not just an ancient anecdote—it is the reality of modern education. Every year, students across the world secure top grades, prestigious careers, and accolades, yet many of them feel empty inside. They have done everything they were told to do, excel in school, get into a reputed university, land a high-paying job. But somewhere along the way, they lost sight of what truly fulfils them.

Many students do not pursue education out of curiosity or passion but because of the promise of status and external validation. They equate success with recognition, a place in the top ranks, an award, a title, a certificate. But once the applause fades, what remains? If knowledge is pursued only for esteem, it never truly nourishes the soul.

The tragedy of esteem-driven education is that it often disconnects students from their true interests and inner calling. Someone who loved art may abandon it for a more "respectable" career. A student with an intuitive mind for philosophy may suppress it in favor of something "practical." Over time, their identity is shaped not by who they are, but by what the world expects them to be.

The Vedanta warns of this illusion, teaching that external validation is fleeting, while true fulfilment comes from self-knowledge. The pursuit of titles, prestige, and accolades may bring temporary satisfaction, but they are like mirages in the desert—visible from afar, yet empty when reached. Real success is not about how the world sees you, but about how deeply you understand yourself.

Socrates' question to Glaucus remains relevant today: Are we truly seeking wisdom, or are we just chasing applause? A student who learns to impress others may achieve much in the world, but a student who learns to understand truth will achieve something far greater: inner fulfilment, clarity, and real wisdom.

Rohan, Jayan, Ravi, Kumar, and Glaucus all faced the same journey—moving from survival to security, from fear to belonging, from success to meaning.

Education must not just teach facts—it must guide students toward wisdom, purpose, and awakening.

The question is: *Are we teaching students to climb the ladder, or are we teaching them to look at the stars?*

Pic: Maslow's Hierarchy of Needs

Reevaluating Maslow: Why Indian Philosophies Offer a More Complete Path to Human Growth

Maslow's Hierarchy of Needs has shaped modern psychology's understanding of human motivation for decades. It has influenced everything from education to corporate structures, reinforcing the belief that growth follows a linear path, from basic survival to self-actualization. At first glance, this model seems logical. It presents a clear roadmap of human progress, suggesting that individuals must first secure their material needs before they can pursue wisdom, creativity, or self-fulfilment. But does growth really follow such a rigid sequence?

Indian thought, particularly Advaita Vedanta, has long rejected this notion. Unlike Maslow's pyramid, which assumes that one must climb step by step, Advaita Vedanta sees human development as something far more fluid. A person need not wait to satisfy their lower needs before seeking higher knowledge. Wisdom, self-awareness, and even enlightenment can emerge at any point in life, regardless of external circumstances. The idea that hunger or insecurity must first be eliminated before an individual can pursue self-inquiry is a materialistic limitation, one that fails to account for the inner journey of the mind and soul.

Advaita Vedanta goes deeper than Maslow in another fundamental way that it does not stop at self-actualization. Maslow's model places self-actualization as the highest state of growth, but even Maslow himself later recognized its limitations (Maslow, A. H. 1969). Toward the end of his life, he acknowledged that self-transcendence was a stage beyond self-actualization, a realization that had already been at the core of Vedantic teachings for thousands of years. The Upanishads, the Bhagavad Gita, and the teachings of Adi Shankaracharya make it clear that true fulfilment is not found in realizing one's personal potential but in dissolving the very sense of self altogether.

This is where Western psychology and Indian philosophy diverge. Maslow sees human development as an accumulation of success, moving from one stage to the next in an orderly fashion. Advaita Vedanta sees it as a shedding of illusion, an unravelling of false identifications with the body, mind, and ego. Maslow suggests that we must build ourselves into something greater. Advaita Vedanta teaches that we must undo everything we believe ourselves to be, until we recognize that we were already limitless from the very beginning.

This is what makes Advaita Vedanta more relevant than ever in today's world. Modern society is obsessed with achievement, with reaching the "top", whether it be in education, career, or personal growth. Students are taught to chase after success, to build their resumes, to prove their worth. But what happens when they get there and still feel empty? The increasing rates of anxiety, depression, and burnout in even the most "successful" individuals show that self-actualization is not enough. What we need is not another system of endless striving but a system of awakening—one that does not keep pushing individuals to "achieve more" but rather guides them toward inner stillness, wisdom, and true fulfilment. (Deutsch, Eliot. 1969)

Advaita Vedanta provides this alternative. It does not deny the importance of material well-being, but it does not make it a prerequisite for self-discovery either. It acknowledges that a person can begin the journey of wisdom at any stage, that fulfilment is not something one reaches at the end of a long climb but something that has always been present, waiting to be recognized. This is why, if we are to reshape education, personal growth, and human motivation, we must shift away from the rigid structures of Maslow's hierarchy and toward the liberating vision of Advaita Vedanta.

To understand this difference through an example, let us turn to the story of Sage Vishwamitra, whose journey from a king to a sage not only reflects Maslow's model but also transcends it, proving that the highest truth is never a matter of accumulation but of surrender.

Sage Vishwamitra's Journey Through Advaita Vedanta

Few stories in Indian mythology portrays the true depth of human transformation as powerfully as the journey of Sage Vishwamitra. His life is not just the tale of a king turned sage, but an symbolism of how human growth transcends material desires, ambition, and even self-actualization, reaching a state far beyond what modern psychology defines. The western psychological models, such as Maslow's Hierarchy of Needs, attempt to categorize human motivation in a linear, structured manner, claiming that individuals must first satisfy basic survival before ascending toward higher understanding. But Vishwamitra's journey, when viewed through the lens of Advaita Vedanta, directly challenges this notion, proving that self-realization is not dependent on external security. Instead, it is an ever-present possibility, accessible at any stage of life, if one chooses to seek it. Unlike Maslow's model, which sees self-actualization as the highest goal, Advaita Vedanta offers a far greater truth, one where human potential does not end with personal fulfilment but dissolves into universal consciousness.

The Hunger for Power: A Material Beginning

Long before he became a revered sage, Vishwamitra was called Kaushika. He was a mighty king, deeply engaged in the concerns of land, wealth, and military strength. His world revolved around expansion and dominance, ensuring that his kingdom remained prosperous and invincible. In this phase, his needs were rooted in material security where he ensured that his people were fed, his armies were strong, and his rule was unchallenged.

Yet, a single encounter would shift the course of his destiny. While on a hunt, he stumbled upon the hermitage of Sage Vashishta, a master of Advaita Vedanta, who lived in the forest with minimal possessions. King Kaushika, accustomed to the grandeur of palaces, was taken aback when he and his entire army were fed and sheltered readily through the divine blessings of Nandini, the celestial cow. He saw in this mystical gift a shortcut to unchallenged prosperity and demanded that Vashishta hand it over.

But true power, Vashishta reminded him, does not lie in possessions. A king may rule the land, but a sage rules the mind. Kaushika, believing himself superior in might, attempted to seize the cow by force. Yet, despite his military strength, he was effortlessly defeated by Vashishta's spiritual power.

It was in that moment of humiliation and defeat that something deeper awakened in Kaushika. His understanding of strength collapsed. His entire life had been spent pursuing material power, yet in front of a sage with nothing, he had been rendered powerless. This realization set him on the first step toward wisdom, not because his physiological and safety needs were fulfilled, as

Maslow's hierarchy might suggest, but because he recognized the limitations of the material world. Advaita Vedanta teaches that all material attachments and worldly pursuits are part of Maya (illusion), which blinds individuals from realizing their true nature. Kaushika had built his entire identity on this illusion of power, and now, for the first time, he began to question it.

The Search for True Strength: A Shift Toward Inner Stability

Kaushika abandoned his kingdom, choosing the path of asceticism. He sought knowledge not out of comfort and abundance but out of a deep existential crisis. This directly counters the assumption that a person must be materially secure before seeking intellectual or spiritual enlightenment. The Upanishads teach that wisdom does not require external stability as true knowledge arises from the ability to look beyond external conditions and into the deeper nature of the self.

Advaita Vedanta does not view human progress as a step-by-step movement from material success to self-realization. Instead, it sees the world as an illusion (Maya), and the only real progress is the ability to detach from this illusion and see the Self (Atman) as one with Brahman (universal consciousness). Kaushika's decision to renounce his throne was not about moving to the next "stage" of growth, it was about rejecting the illusion that material power was ever real in the first place.

The Temptation of Love and Recognition

Even as an ascetic, Kaushika was not yet free from the desire for validation. His penance was intense, his mastery over spiritual forces immense, but his ego still sought acknowledgment from the gods, the sages, and the celestial realms. This reflects the common trap of learning for prestige rather than true understanding.

When Indra sent Menaka, the celestial apsara, to distract him, Kaushika, despite his discipline, fell into the illusion of companionship and worldly pleasure. He spent years with Menaka, believing himself to have found peace. But eventually, realization struck, and understood that his sense of fulfilment was conditional, dependent on external love and approval.

Advaita Vedanta teaches that attachment, even to love, is a binding force. It is another form of Maya that keeps the mind entangled in the material world. Kaushika's wisdom deepened not when he received love, but when he saw through its transience. He left Menaka, not out of bitterness, but because he understood that attachment to relationships, however beautiful, could not replace the ultimate truth he sought.

Breaking the Ego: From Esteem to Wisdom

Even after centuries of meditation, Kaushika still longed for recognition. He returned to Vashishta, demanding that he now be acknowledged as a Brahmarishi, the highest title for a sage. But true wisdom does not seek acknowledgment.

Vashishta did not respond, knowing that so long as Kaushika needed external validation, he had not yet arrived at true realization. This moment reflects one of the greatest dangers in modern education, the belief that knowledge is proven through degrees, titles, and awards. Many students, like Kaushika, at this stage, do not learn for wisdom; they learn to be recognized as wise.

Beyond Self-Actualization: The Path to Transcendence

When Kaushika finally let go of the need for acknowledgment, something within him dissolved. He no longer sought power, recognition, or external validation. At that moment, Vashishta smiled and named him Vishwamitra, "the friend of the universe." He had not just achieved self-actualization, as Maslow might define it, he had transcended the self entirely.

This is the essence of Advaita Vedanta that self-actualization is not the highest goal because the very idea of the "self" is an illusion. True wisdom is not found in achieving personal greatness but in dissolving the false identity that keeps one bound to material existence. The Upanishads, Bhagavad Gita, and the teachings of Adi Shankaracharya all emphasize that the final stage of growth is not self-fulfilment but self-transcendence, the realization that the self is Brahman, infinite and boundless.

The Lesson for Modern Education

Modern education, much like Maslow's hierarchy, remains trapped in the illusion of external achievement. Schools emphasize grades, careers, and material stability while ignoring the deeper aspects of wisdom, ethics, and inner growth. If we truly want an education system that nurtures complete human beings, we must move past Western psychological models and embrace the teachings of Advaita Vedanta, which recognize that knowledge is not just about reaching personal success but about awakening to the ultimate reality. The point of argument here is not against the concept of Maslow's hierarchy, but against that fact that its rigidity might not be ideal when reflecting on the true purpose of education. Hence, its time that we think beyond this, and incorporate the Indian way of life, as it delivers us a more focused and meaningful objective towards understanding and achieving goals beyond self-actualisation – Transcendence. Isn't the true purpose of education liberation? In Tagore's words, "Where the mind the without fear and the head is held high..." (Tagore, 1912)

Vishwamitra's story, somewhere nudges us deep inside and teaches us that the highest form of education is not about climbing a hierarchy, it is about transcending it altogether. If we are to reclaim true education, we must move beyond producing achievers and start nurturing awakened minds.

Pic: Advaita Vedanta: A way of life.

BLOOM'S TAXONOMY AND INTELLECTUAL EVOLUTION

The Progression of Learning: From Knowledge to Wisdom

Throughout history, education has often been reduced to the mechanical transmission of knowledge. Schools, universities, and institutions have primarily functioned as repositories of information, emphasizing the memorization and reproduction of facts rather than the development of wisdom. However, I would like to reiterate this idea once again that true learning is not about accumulation, it is about transformation. A person may know every scientific principle, every law, every scripture, but if they cannot apply, analyze, or evolve beyond this knowledge, then learning remains incomplete and ineffective.

This idea is at the core of Bloom's Taxonomy. This is a framework proposed by Benjamin Bloom in 1956 that outlines the hierarchy of cognitive development. This framework has been the

Bible for teachers for many years. According to Bloom, learning progresses through six distinct stages, each representing a higher level of intellectual mastery:

1. Remembering – The ability to recall facts, definitions, and concepts.
2. Understanding – Grasping meaning, interpreting information, and explaining ideas.
3. Applying – Using knowledge in practical scenarios, problem-solving, and real-world application.
4. Analyzing – Examining relationships, identifying patterns, and drawing deeper connections.
5. Evaluating – Forming independent judgments, critiquing ideas, and making reasoned decisions.
6. Creating – Innovating, synthesizing new knowledge, and generating original thought.

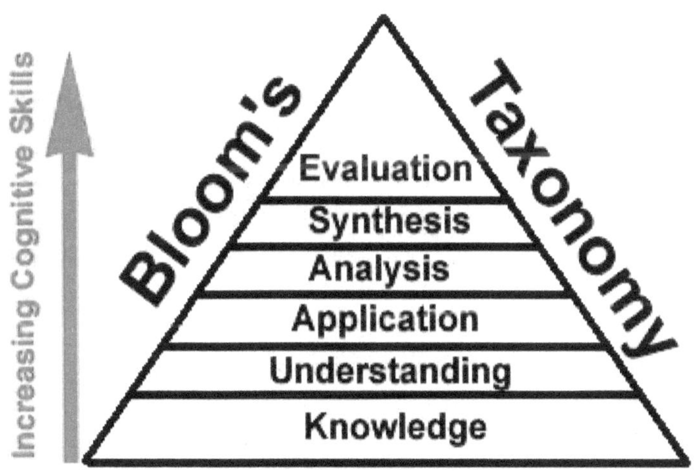

Pic: Bloom's Taxonomy Model

Education is often seen as a ladder, where students move from one level to the next and they are meant to master each stage before they progress. But learning is rarely so structured in real life. It happens in layers, sometimes moving forward, sometimes looping back, shaped by curiosity, experience, and self-discovery. However, looking back at Bloom's Taxonomy that has widely been used in education, I have attempted to map this process with simple examples that defines the six levels of learning: Remembering, Understanding, Applying, Analyzing, Evaluating, and Creating.

At its core, Bloom's model is meant to guide students from passive knowledge to active mastery, but how does it actually unfold in today's world? Let's consider a high school student, Maya, who is passionate about environmental science. She begins her learning journey just like every student, by absorbing information, but what happens as she moves through the levels of Bloom's Taxonomy?

At first, Maya learns through **Remembering**. She memorizes definitions, what climate change is, the causes of global warming, and the key scientific terms. She can list the greenhouse gases, recall data about rising temperatures, and repeat what her textbooks say. But at this stage, knowledge remains static. She can answer quiz questions, but she does not yet grasp the bigger picture.

When she moves to **Understanding**, things begin to shift. She no longer just recalls facts, she starts explaining them. She realizes that climate change is not just about melting ice caps but about human choices, economic policies, and long-term consequences. She can now put ideas into her own words, articulate why fossil fuels contribute to global warming, and discuss how deforestation impacts biodiversity. But even now, her learning is still theoretical.

It is only when Maya reaches **Applying** that learning becomes meaningful. She takes what she knows and uses it in the real world. Maybe she starts a small project to track her school's carbon footprint. She calculates how much energy is wasted, proposes solutions to reduce electricity use, and sees the practical impact of her knowledge. Unlike before, where facts existed in isolation, she now understands how they intersect with real-life actions.

But true mastery requires more than just applying knowledge, it demands **Analyzing.** Maya begins to compare different climate policies, noticing patterns in how governments approach environmental regulations. She examines why some countries invest in renewable energy while others rely on coal. She no longer just accepts solutions at face value, she questions them, breaks them down, and looks at hidden complexities.

This deeper thinking leads her to **Evaluating**. She no longer just gathers information now, she critiques it. When she reads news articles about sustainability, she questions their sources, weighs evidence, and forms her own judgment. Is carbon offsetting an effective solution, or is it just a way for corporations to continue polluting? Should developing nations be held to the same environmental standards as industrialized countries? At this level, Maya does not just accept what she is taught but engages in independent thought.

Finally, the highest stage is **Creating**. Here, Maya no longer just consumes knowledge. She produces it. Perhaps she develops an innovative campaign to raise awareness about plastic waste, writes a research paper proposing a new policy for urban sustainability, or designs an app that helps individuals reduce their environmental impact. She is no longer just a student, she is a thinker, an innovator, and a contributor.

This journey, from passive memorization to active creation, is what Bloom's Taxonomy envisions. But in reality, most education systems stop students at the lower levels. Too often, learning remains trapped in rote memorization and surface-level understanding (Lower Order Thinking), never pushing students toward analysis, evaluation, and creative thought (Higher Order Thinking). Maya's journey is an ideal one, but for many students, this path is obstructed by rigid curriculums, standardized tests, and an overemphasis on results rather than depth of thought.

In today's world, where information is readily available, remembering facts is no longer enough. Artificial Intelligence can now store, process, and recall data faster than any human. The real question for today's students is not "What do you know?" but "What can you do with what you know?" The purpose of education must be to move beyond knowledge acquisition and towards knowledge application, critical thinking, and innovation.

Although Bloom's Taxonomy still remains a valuable guide today, but it is not the final destination, it cannot be. True learning is not just about climbing an intellectual ladder but about developing the ability to think deeply, act wisely, and create meaning in an ever-changing world, and this is where the Indian perspective of Upanishads comes in.

Beyond Knowledge: The Indian Perspective on Intellectual Evolution

The Indian philosophical tradition provides a parallel framework for understanding human cognition and self-awareness. The Taittiriya Upanishad (2.1-5) describe the five koshas (sheaths), which represent different layers of consciousness, similar to how Bloom's Taxonomy describes progressive levels of intellectual mastery.

1. Annamaya Kosha (Physical Sheath) – The most basic level, focused on bodily needs and survival.
2. Pranamaya Kosha (Energy Sheath) – The layer of cognitive awareness, emotions, and instinctive learning.
3. Manomaya Kosha (Mind Sheath) – The domain of thought, memory, and conditioned mental patterns.
4. Vijnanamaya Kosha (Wisdom Sheath) – The stage of higher reasoning, analysis, and judgment.
5. Anandamaya Kosha (Bliss Sheath) – The state of pure wisdom and self-realization.

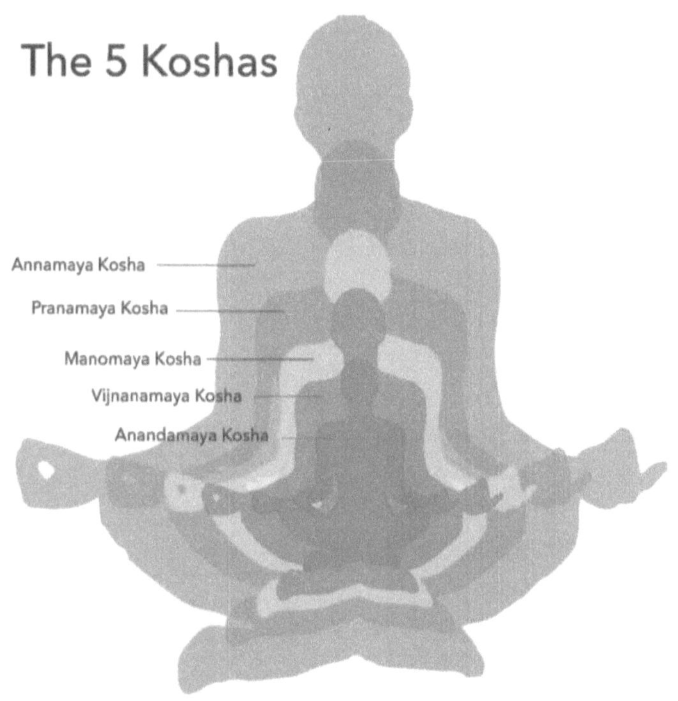

Pic: The 5 Koshas of Taittiriya Upanishad

In order to fully understand how learning progresses from mechanical knowledge to higher wisdom, it is necessary that we examine the connection between Bloom's Taxonomy and the five koshas (sheaths of human consciousness) described in Upanishadic philosophy. These koshas provide a spiritual model of cognitive and existential development, representing the six levels of intellectual evolution proposed in Bloom's framework.

Just as Bloom's Taxonomy describes the hierarchy of learning, the koshas describe the layers of human awareness, moving from the most basic survival instincts to ultimate self-realization.

In the process of breaking down the Koshas and Bloom's Taxonomy, I have observed a striking similarity between the basics of these two ideas. The lower stages of learning, i.e. Remembering, Understanding, and Applying, are associated with the first three koshas, where cognition is largely mechanical, reactive, and conditioned by external factors. Whereas, the higher stages of learning, i.e. Analyzing, Evaluating, and Creating, correspond to the last two koshas, where knowledge transforms into deep insight, critical thinking, and creative mastery.

To make this easier to grasp, let's explore each kosha in relation to Bloom's Taxonomy with some stories and mythological references paired with modern educational insights.

I. Annamaya Kosha (The Physical Sheath) – The Foundation of Learning

Bloom's Level: Remembering

The Annamaya Kosha is the most basic layer of human existence, associated with physical survival, sensory experience, and bodily needs. In the context of learning, this is the stage where education is purely mechanical, focused on memorization and repetition without deeper comprehension. Consider a student who is preparing for a history exam. He memorizes dates, names, and facts, repeating them like a mantra. However, when asked to explain why the French Revolution happened or what its consequences were, he is unable to answer. At this stage, learning is purely passive as the information is absorbed but not truly processed.

The story of Ekalavya from The Mahabharata is known to most of us. However, it is interesting to observe that how it serves as a striking example of how learning, when confined to memorization, remains incomplete. A boy with a deep passion for archery, Ekalavya was denied formal education under Dronacharya, the royal teacher of the Pandavas and Kauravas. Undeterred, he crafted a statue of Dronacharya and practiced in front of it, believing that devotion and repetition would make him a great archer. Through sheer determination, he memorized techniques, mastered precise movements, and became exceptionally skilled. Yet, despite his talent, his learning remained unquestioned and untested in real battle. He had reached only the first stage of learning - Remembering. Here, we would not delve into the deeper connotations of this story, but the understanding that dialogue and enquiry is necessary in education, without which a student may master the prescribed education but would never be able to attend true wisdom. This is the same challenge that many modern students face in education systems that emphasize rote learning over conceptual understanding. Students may recall multiplication tables, chemical formulas, or historical dates with precision, but without context, analysis, and application, their learning remains mechanical rather than meaningful.

In most classrooms, even today, memorization is often mistaken for mastery. Learning must move beyond simple recall to deeper levels of understanding, application, and critical thinking. Without this transition, education becomes a ritual of repetition rather than a journey of discovery. The starting story of Ekalavya should remind us that knowledge, if not tested, challenged, and expanded upon, remains incomplete, fragile, and ultimately limited in its power.

II. Pranamaya Kosha (The Energy Sheath) – Developing Understanding

Bloom's Level: Understanding

The Pranamaya Kosha is the layer of cognition, energy, and emotion. It corresponds to the Understanding stage in Bloom's Taxonomy, where the student begins to grasp meaning rather than just recall information. A student who remembers Newton's Laws of Motion at the previous level now asks, "What do these laws mean?" She understands that the First Law explains inertia, and the Third Law describes action and reaction forces. She is no longer just memorizing words but seeing their logical connections and implications.

Looking back at our mythology, in the Ramayana, Hanuman initially forgets his divine strength due to a curse in childhood. He functions at a basic level, unaware of his potential. However, when Jambavan reminds him of his abilities, Hanuman suddenly understands his true power. He is no longer just a warrior but a force of divine energy. This moment can be seen as a student moving from passive memory to realization, the first step toward intellectual and personal evolution.

Many students in today's times can recite passages from Shakespeare's Hamlet with perfect accuracy, but when asked to interpret its deeper themes, they struggle. They may recall famous lines like "To be, or not to be," yet fail to grasp the existential dilemma that haunts Hamlet throughout the play. Memorization alone does not lead to insight; it merely stores information without fostering real engagement. True learning begins when students move beyond word-for-word recall and start to question, analyze, and connect literature to their own experiences. Understanding allows them to see Hamlet's internal conflict as a reflection of human uncertainty, his hesitation as a symbol of moral struggle, and his fate as a consequence of unresolved emotion. When students engage with knowledge at this level, education becomes more than just a process of accumulation, it transforms into an exploration of meaning, self-awareness, and intellectual curiosity.

III. Manomaya Kosha (The Mind Sheath) – Applying Knowledge

Bloom's Level: Applying

The Manomaya Kosha is the layer of thought, conditioned beliefs, and mental processing. It corresponds to Applying in Bloom's Taxonomy, where the learner actively uses knowledge instead of just storing it. A student who has memorized electrical circuits (Remembering) and understands how they work (Understanding) now applies that knowledge by designing a working circuit. This is a significant shift, where education becomes experiential rather than theoretical.

Again, looking back at the story of Arjun from The Mahabharata, we can say that Arjun does not just study archery, he applies it in real scenarios. His Guru, Dronacharya, challenges him to shoot moving targets, practice blindfolded, and master focus in combat situations. Arjun, in Mahabharata, reaches the Applying stage where his knowledge is repeatedly seen to be transformed into practical skill.

A student who memorizes grammar rules and sentence structures but struggles to write fluently remains stuck at the Understanding stage. They may know the technicalities of subject-verb agreement, tenses, and punctuation, yet when asked to express thoughts clearly on paper, they hesitate. Their knowledge exists in theory but lacks real-world application. Similarly, a medical student who has extensively studied anatomy, memorized every muscle and nerve, and excelled in written exams, is not yet a surgeon. Until they have performed an actual surgery, their learning remains incomplete. True mastery begins only when knowledge is put into practice, tested through experience, and adapted to real-life challenges. The shift from Understanding to Applying is what separates those who simply know from those who can do, create, and innovate.

IV. Vijnanamaya Kosha (The Wisdom Sheath) – Higher-Order Thinking

Bloom's Level: Analyzing & Evaluating

The Vijnanamaya Kosha represents wisdom, intuition, and self-awareness. It corresponds to the Analyzing and Evaluating stages of Bloom's Taxonomy, where students critically examine concepts, form independent judgments, and engage in deep intellectual inquiry. A student studying Plato's Allegory of the Cave now compares it to modern media influence, analyzing how perception shapes reality. She begins to evaluate knowledge instead of blindly accepting it.

Again, referring to the third Pandava Arjun, we see how he was overwhelmed by doubt in the battlefield of Kurukshetra and when Krishna delivers the discourse of Bhagavat Gita to him, he does not just receive the wisdom, he questions, reflects, and debates. This critical thinking aligns with Vijnanamaya Kosha where true wisdom emerges when one evaluates knowledge deeply, rather than accepting it blindly.

Universities should not only focus on what to learn but also on how to think, question, and evaluate knowledge critically. In an era where information is abundant and easily accessible, memorizing facts is no longer enough—students must develop the ability to analyze sources, challenge assumptions, and form independent judgments. This level of learning extends beyond academics into ethical decision-making, leadership, and philosophy, where answers are not always absolute. A future leader must not only understand policies but also weigh their moral implications. A philosopher must not only study ideas but also refine them through logic and debate. This is the stage where education moves beyond the accumulation of knowledge and begins to cultivate wisdom, discernment, and the ability to navigate complexity with clarity and ethical responsibility.

V. Anandamaya Kosha (The Bliss Sheath) – The Creation of New Knowledge

Bloom's Level: Creating

The Anandamaya Kosha is the highest level of consciousness, representing pure awareness, innovation, and self-mastery. It corresponds to Creating in Bloom's Taxonomy, where knowledge is synthesized, transformed, and applied to create new ideas. Einstein did not just memorize physics, he created new theories that reshaped our understanding of the universe.

And, in this context, if we look back to our mythology, we will find innumerable examples that would validate this idea. Veda Vyasa did not just recite existing scriptures, he composed the

Mahabharata, bringing together knowledge from different traditions to create something profoundly original.

Creativity is the pinnacle of learning, where students move beyond absorbing knowledge and begin to generate new ideas, innovate, and push boundaries. At this level, they no longer rely solely on existing frameworks but instead question, experiment, and create something original. Whether composing a symphony, designing groundbreaking technology, or developing a fresh perspective in philosophy, learners at this stage transform knowledge into something uniquely their own. True mastery is not just about understanding or applying what has been taught, it is about reimagining, reshaping, and contributing to the ever-evolving body of human knowledge.

The Path from Memory to Mastery

The journey from Annamaya Kosha to Anandamaya Kosha reiterates the progression in Bloom's Taxonomy, but in a more profound manner, guiding us with the pathway from mechanical learning to wisdom and innovation.

Here, the question arises yet again. Are we teaching students to merely recall facts, or are we guiding them to create, innovate, and awaken?

True education is not just about knowing more - it is about becoming more.

The Koshas
annamaya kosha
pranamaya kosha
manomaya kosha
vijnanamaya kosha
anandamaya kosha
SELF
bliss
discernment
mind
energy
food
Kosha — sheath

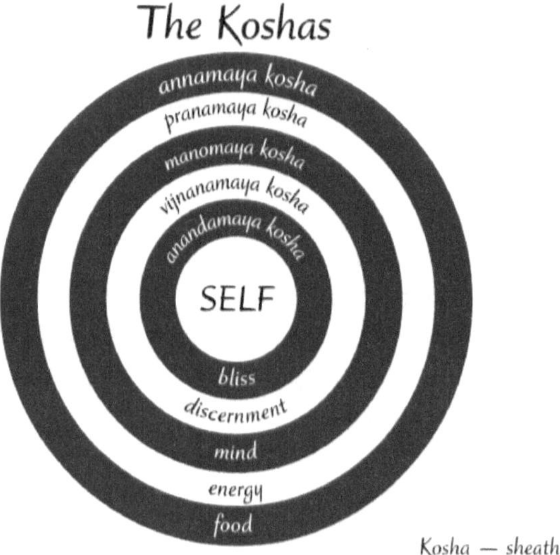

Pic: Koshas

Wisdom from The Mahabharata: Drawing a Philosophical Contrast Between Karna and Arjun

When discussing about the difference between what more needs to be done in our education system than what is already happening, I cannot help but recall the epic story of The Mahabharata repeatedly. Let's just look at this philosophical masterpiece from a perspective beyond religion. The Mahabharata is often read as a tale of war, destiny, and cosmic justice, but beneath its epic battles and divine interventions, it is a profound study of human learning, self-awareness, and intellectual evolution. Two of its central characters, Karna and Arjun, somewhere stand as embodiments of contrasting approaches to knowledge and wisdom.

Both warriors were equally gifted, highly trained, and immensely powerful, yet their fates could not have been more different. Arjun rose to the height of wisdom and mastery, while Karna remained bound by his limitations, unable to transcend the burdens of fate. This contrast is not merely a reflection of external circumstances but of their individual approaches to learning, self-improvement, and the pursuit of true knowledge.

This case study will examine why Karna, although being one of my personal favourite characters from the Mahabharata, faltered despite his formidable skills and why Arjun succeeded where Karna failed. To do so, we will map their journeys onto Taittiriya Upanishad and support the analysis with references from the Bhagavad Gita, Samkhya philosophy, and Vedantic teachings.

Arjun's journey progressed through all the stages of education as discussed earlier, ultimately reaching the highest level of wisdom. Karna, however, remained trapped in the lower and middle stages, unable to rise beyond his conditioned attachments and emotions. Let's examine how.

Both Karna and Arjun began their learning journeys in a similar manner, receiving training under great masters. Karna studied under Parashurama, the greatest teacher of warfare, while Arjun was trained by Dronacharya, the guru of the Kuru princes. Karna was an exceptionally talented student. He had always demonstrated phenomenal recall and mastery of complex battle techniques, divine mantras, and celestial weapon invocations. He memorized the intricacies of warfare, from the Shastras (scriptures of combat) to the Vyuhas (battle formations), and was considered one of the most skilled warriors of his time.

However, Karna's knowledge remained mechanical. He learned through rote memorization to a lot extent rather than internalization and self-reflection. His approach was focused on acquiring power and proving his worth, rather than deeply contemplating the ethical and strategic implications of warfare.

Arjun, in contrast, did not stop at memorization. Under Dronacharya, he constantly refined and questioned what he learned, seeking a deeper understanding of strategy, dharma, and the philosophy of warfare.

This distinction is crucial in Samkhya philosophy, which differentiates between "smriti" (memory-based knowledge) and "buddhi" (intellect-based knowledge). Karna excelled in smriti, accumulating vast amounts of information, but never progressed toward buddhi, which allows for independent thinking, critical evaluation, and deeper wisdom.

Karna's greatest failure was his inability to understand the true purpose of his learning. Though he possessed immense technical knowledge, he never analyzed the ethical responsibilities that came with it. This flaw is revealed in his blind loyalty to Duryodhana. Karna justified his allegiance as an act of gratitude, but he never evaluated whether Duryodhana's cause was truly just. Despite knowing that the Kauravas acted out of adharma (unrighteousness), Karna refused to question his role, seeing himself as a victim of fate rather than an agent of moral choice.

In the Bhagavad Gita, Krishna emphasizes that true wisdom comes from acting with understanding, not blind adherence to duty:

"A wise man does not act out of mechanical habit but from conscious understanding." (Gita 2.50)

Arjun, on the other hand, constantly questioned his actions. When he was granted the Pashupatastra by Lord Shiva, he did not simply accept it, he asked when and how it should be used, under what conditions, and with what responsibility. His inquiries showed that he understood knowledge as a tool of dharma, not just power.

The true test of knowledge is not in theory but in application. Karna possessed all the technical expertise of a warrior, yet when his chariot wheel got stuck in the battlefield, he panicked and forgot the mantras to invoke his divine weapons. Many attribute this to Parashurama's curse, but one can always argue that the deeper reality could be that Karna had never internalized his learning at a subconscious level. He relied on external validation and fixed techniques rather than developing an instinctual mastery of his craft.

Arjun, in contrast, faced his own moment of crisis where he encountered self-hesitation before the battle. But unlike Karna, he turned to self-inquiry and wisdom. Through Krishna's teachings in the Bhagavad Gita, he transformed his knowledge into decisive action.

Krishna instructs Arjun:

"Perform your duty with a steady mind, free from attachment to success or failure." (Gita 2.47)

This philosophy, Karma Yoga (the path of detached action), which was later elaborated by Swami Vivekananda (1896), allowed Arjun to move beyond fear, doubt, and hesitation, while Karna remained paralyzed by circumstances.

Arjun eventually progressed to higher stages of Bloom's Taxonomy, or we can say the higher sheaths of the Kosha Structure.

He analyzed the meaning of dharma, understood that his duty was not personal but cosmic, and ultimately developed his own ethical framework for battle.

Karna, on the other hand, remained attached to his emotions, grudges, and personal conflicts. He never questioned:

- Why Duryodhana supported him.
- Whether his loyalty was misplaced.
- If his understanding of honour was truly aligned with dharma.

"He who sees action in inaction, and inaction in action, is truly wise." (Gita 4.18)

Arjun saw beyond war; he recognized his role in the cosmic balance of dharma. Karna, however, remained imprisoned by his unexamined fate.

What Education Must Learn from Karna's Fate

Hence, it can be referred on a surface level (because we are not really delving further deeper into the great philosophical world of The Mahabharata in fear for the plausibility of losing context), that Karna did not fail due to lack of intelligence or talent, he failed because his learning remained incomplete. He never evolved beyond mechanical knowledge into self-awareness and higher wisdom.

Arjun, however, transcended the lower levels of learning and moved toward intellectual independence, self-mastery, and enlightened action.

This case study serves as a critical warning for education today. If we train students only in memorization and technical skills, we will produce Karnas, intelligent but unprepared for life's real challenges. Education must not only teach knowledge but also cultivate wisdom, self-awareness, and ethical decision-making.

So, the question is: Are We Training Students to Be Karna or Arjuna?

If we fail to move beyond rote learning and technical mastery, we will create a generation of highly skilled but directionless individuals. True education must create awakened minds, not just knowledgeable individuals. For in the end, the greatest test of learning is not what we remember, but how we evolve.

Beyond Bloom's Taxonomy: Why Education Needs the Indian Kosha System

For decades, Bloom's Taxonomy has served as a guiding framework in education, shaping how teachers design curricula and assess learning. It provides a structured, step-by-step approach to intellectual development, moving from basic recall of knowledge to higher-order thinking skills such as evaluation and creation. It has undoubtedly contributed to modern pedagogy, helping educators focus on fostering critical thinking rather than just rote memorization. However, in today's world, where artificial intelligence, automation, and rapidly changing knowledge landscapes are redefining learning itself, Bloom's model is no longer enough.

Bloom's Taxonomy is primarily a cognitive model, structured around how students process and apply information. While it accounts for intellectual growth, it does not deeply address the emotional, ethical, and spiritual dimensions of learning, aspects that are crucial in an age where mental well-being, adaptability, and deeper wisdom are more important than ever. The Indian knowledge tradition, particularly the Kosha System from Taittiriya Upanishad, offers a far more holistic, time-tested, and superior model, the kind that does not just train the intellect but nurtures the entire human being - mind, body, and spirit.

The Limitations of Bloom's Taxonomy

Bloom's model is sequential and compartmentalized. It assumes that learning progresses in a structured, stepwise manner, from simple recall to complex creativity. However, real learning does not always happen in a straight line. Creativity is not necessarily the final stage of learning, it can often come at the very beginning, even before deep analysis. A poet, for instance, may intuitively compose a profound piece of work without consciously "analyzing" poetic forms beforehand. Similarly, a scientist may envision a breakthrough before systematically understanding its components.

Moreover, Bloom's taxonomy remains bound to the Western tradition of rationality and compartmentalized knowledge, whereas Indian philosophy recognizes that learning is an integration of intellect, experience, and inner consciousness. Knowledge is not just about analyzing facts, it is about understanding oneself and the universe at a fundamental level.

In today's world, education cannot just be about cognitive intelligence. It must include emotional resilience, ethical clarity, self-awareness, and inner balance. This is where the Kosha system of ancient Indian philosophy becomes not only relevant but indispensable.

Why the Kosha System Offers a Superior Alternative

The journey of learning is not a linear path of accumulating information but a transformative process that shapes the entire human being, physically, emotionally, intellectually, and spiritually. While Bloom's Taxonomy has long guided educational structures by categorizing learning into hierarchical stages, its scope remains largely confined to the cognitive areas. It emphasizes recall, comprehension, and critical thinking, progressing toward evaluation and creation. This model has undoubtedly contributed to pedagogical advancements, but it remains incomplete. The ancient Indian Kosha system, on the other hand, recognizes that true learning is not limited to the intellect. It is an integration of the body, mind, energy, wisdom, and consciousness. Unlike Bloom's model, which views education as an intellectual exercise, the Kosha system sees it as a holistic unfolding of human potential.

Modern education, following Bloom's principles, primarily engages with what can be measured, tested, and quantified. It mostly focuses on external knowledge rather than internal transformation. However, the limitations of this approach become apparent when we consider real-life learning. A student may master the highest levels of Bloom's framework, analyzing complex problems, evaluating theories, and even creating new models, yet still struggle with mental clarity, emotional stability, and a sense of purpose. A brilliant scientist may excel in critical thinking but remain burdened by stress and discontent. A skilled entrepreneur may innovate endlessly yet lack the wisdom to navigate life's deeper existential questions. Bloom's taxonomy does not address these aspects because it is limited to cognitive progression, while the Kosha system accounts for the entire spectrum of human learning and self-awareness.

Where Bloom's Taxonomy structures learning as a progression from basic to advanced cognition, the Kosha system understands that different aspects of human awareness unfold simultaneously and influence one another. It does not separate knowledge acquisition from emotional intelligence or wisdom from well-being. A student's physical health and mental state deeply affect their ability to learn, and no level of intellectual mastery can compensate for an education that neglects these elements. This is why in ancient Gurukul systems, learning was never just about memorizing scriptures or debating logic, it was about building character, aligning thought with ethical understanding, and cultivating inner stillness. Unlike the fragmented Western approach, which often separates knowledge into disciplines, the Kosha system fosters interconnected learning, where mathematics, philosophy, the arts, and self-reflection are not distinct subjects but threads of the same fabric.

Another significant limitation of Bloom's model is that it assumes learning follows a fixed sequence and that students must first master lower levels before progressing to higher ones. But real education is often nonlinear. Insights can come in moments of deep intuition before conscious understanding. A child may display profound creative abilities even before grasping fundamental theories. A musician may compose a masterpiece without ever formally analyzing musical structures. Learning does not always begin with remembering facts and end with creation. It can emerge from an intuitive realization and later be structured through logic. The Kosha system acknowledges this fluidity of intellectual and spiritual growth, understanding that different aspects of learning can be activated at different times depending on the individual's journey.

Moreover, Bloom's model culminates in creation as the highest form of intellectual achievement. But what happens beyond that? The Kosha system recognizes that true learning does not end at mastery of knowledge but moves toward wisdom and transcendence. While Bloom's taxonomy stops at intellectual success, the Kosha framework encourages self-inquiry, ethical clarity, and the realization that knowledge must ultimately serve a greater purpose. It shifts the focus from achievement to awakening, from simply producing thinkers to nurturing enlightened individuals.

Education today desperately needs this shift. In an era where AI can analyze, evaluate, and even create, Bloom's taxonomy alone is no longer enough. Machines can now perform cognitive tasks at levels beyond human capability, raising a critical question: If thinking, analyzing, and even innovating can be automated, what remains uniquely human? The answer lies in what the Kosha system has always recognized—true learning is not just about information processing but about cultivating wisdom, emotional intelligence, ethical decision-making, and ultimately, self-realization.

The modern world, despite its advancements, is witnessing a crisis of meaning. Students graduate with knowledge but lack clarity. Professionals reach the heights of their careers yet remain unfulfilled. Anxiety, stress, and mental health struggles plague even the most accomplished individuals. If education is to truly evolve, it must move beyond Bloom's cognitive framework and embrace a model that nurtures the entire human experience. The Kosha system does not reject intellectual learning, it expands it, integrating mind, body, and spirit into one unified process. It is not just a framework for education; it is a blueprint for lifelong transformation.

This is why the rebranding of the Kosha system is crucial for the future of education. It must not be dismissed as an ancient spiritual concept but recognized as a scientifically aligned, psychologically valid, and urgently needed educational model. It is time to bridge ancient wisdom with modern pedagogy, to ensure that education does not just create skilled professionals but conscious individuals who can navigate the complexities of life with clarity, purpose, and wisdom.

Rebranding the Kosha System: A Modern Education Model

In today's rapidly evolving world, education cannot afford to remain bound by outdated frameworks that focus solely on cognitive learning. The Kosha system, deeply rooted in Vedantic philosophy and holistic wisdom, offers an advanced educational model that modern pedagogy desperately needs. Unlike Bloom's Taxonomy, which isolates intellectual growth from emotional and spiritual development, the Kosha system acknowledges the interconnectedness of all aspects of human existence. It does not separate the mind from the body, knowledge from wisdom, or intelligence from consciousness. Instead, it integrates them into a singular journey of lifelong transformation.

For too long, Indian knowledge traditions have been dismissed as esoteric or unscientific, yet modern neuroscience and psychology now validate what Vedanta taught thousands of years ago, that learning is not just a function of memory and analysis but of emotional balance, self-awareness, and deep engagement with the world. Research in cognitive neuroscience has demonstrated that higher-order thinking is directly influenced by emotional and physiological states (Damasio, 1994). Students struggling with stress, anxiety, or lack of purpose cannot truly engage in deep learning. The Upanishads, however, recognized this long before modern science, stating that "only when the mind is still, wisdom arises" (Katha Upanishad 2.3.10).

Even in Western thought, pioneers of education and psychology have acknowledged the limitations of purely intellectual education. Albert Einstein once said, "Education is not the learning of facts, but the training of the mind to think" (Einstein, 1954). But what does it mean to truly "train the mind"? It is not just about sharpening intelligence; it is about cultivating depth of thought, ethical reasoning, and an ability to see beyond surface-level knowledge. This is exactly what the Kosha system offers, an education that is not just skill-oriented but wisdom-driven.

Swami Vivekananda, one of India's most profound thinkers, argued that true education is not about feeding the brain with information but about awakening the soul (Vivekananda, 1897). He emphasized that "education must be man-making", meaning that it should develop character, resilience, and self-awareness, not just prepare individuals for jobs. This contrasts sharply with today's industrialized education system, which remains largely a continuation of the colonial framework designed to produce efficient workers rather than enlightened individuals (Guha, 2008). The Kosha system, if integrated into modern pedagogy, has the potential to restore this lost depth and purpose in education.

Why This Shift is the Need of the Hour

Our world today is immensely dominated by artificial intelligence, automation, and existential uncertainty. Thus, our education system must prepare students for more than just academic excellence. It must equip them with the ability to navigate complexity, develop emotional intelligence, and cultivate wisdom. AI can now analyze, evaluate, and even create, tasks once considered the peak of human cognition under Bloom's Taxonomy. But AI lacks the ability to reflect, to exercise ethical judgment, to understand human emotions, and to seek meaning beyond data. If students are trained only within the cognitive boundaries of Bloom's model, they risk becoming competent but directionless, knowledgeable but unwise, intelligent but incapable of true insight.

The Bhagavad Gita (2.50) states that "a wise person does not act merely for personal gain but with clarity and a vision beyond the self." If education is to remain relevant in the age of AI, it must emphasize self-awareness, ethical reasoning, and higher consciousness—areas where machines cannot compete. The Kosha system, unlike Bloom's rigid framework, does not limit learning to mental functions alone but extends it to the emotional, ethical, and spiritual realms, making it a far more sustainable and future-proof model.

Rabindranath Tagore envisioned an education system that nurtured creativity, self-expression, and connection to the larger human experience (Tagore, 1917). His school, Shantiniketan, was an attempt to break free from colonial education's mechanical structure and introduce an organic, holistic approach to learning, one that aligned closely with the Kosha system. Yet, a century later, most educational systems worldwide remain trapped in the same industrialized, test-oriented framework that prioritizes academic performance over intellectual liberation.

If we truly wish to reform education, we must move beyond fragmented Western models and reintroduce the Kosha system as a scientifically sound, psychologically valid, and spiritually enriching educational framework. This is not about rejecting Bloom's model, it is about going beyond it, integrating it into a wider, deeper understanding of learning that accounts for the entire human experience.

The greatest minds in history - Einstein, Tagore, Vivekananda, have all emphasized that education should not just fill minds but free them. The time has come to reclaim our own traditions, to rebrand the Kosha system for modern use, and to implement a model of education that does not just create professionals but awakened individuals. Because in the end, education should not be about training the intellect alone—it should be about liberating the whole being.

84

THE NEED FOR A HOLISTIC APPROACH TO EDUCATION

The Story of Bharadwaja's Unfinished Learning

You might have heard of Rishi Bharadwaja, one of the Sapta Rishis, a sage whose thirst for knowledge was unending. His story is found in the Mahabharata as a tale of a man who dedicated his entire life to learning. He memorized the Vedas, meditated for years, and spent every waking moment in deep study, believing that the more he knew, the closer he would be to ultimate wisdom. Yet, when he reached old age, he realized that he had only scratched the surface of wisdom. As the legend goes, Lord Indra appeared before him and, seeing Bharadwaja's relentless pursuit of knowledge, granted him a divine vision.

Indra pointed to three great mountains and said, *"O Sage, the knowledge you have gathered in this lifetime is but a handful of dust compared to the vastness of wisdom, as these three mountains stand before you. Learning is infinite, but true wisdom is not just in knowing—it is in living, experiencing, and realizing the essence of knowledge."*

This story can be seen as a powerful metaphor for modern education. Today, we have more information than ever before, with endless books, digital resources, and institutional degrees. Yet, like Bharadwaja, if we focus only on intellectual accumulation without deeper experiential and spiritual realization, our learning remains incomplete.

Holistic education is not just about academic excellence, it cannot be. Holistic education is about intellectual, emotional, and spiritual growth. It is about ensuring that learning is not confined to memory and logic but extends to experience, introspection, and self-awareness.

In an earlier chapter, we discussed the story of Nachiketa, a seeker who realized that true wisdom is not in rituals but in self-inquiry. That discussion illustrated how education should encourage students to move beyond passive knowledge toward deep realization.

Now, we take this idea further, what does it truly mean to integrate intellectual, emotional, and spiritual learning? How can education bridge these dimensions to create individuals who are not just informed but also awakened?

This chapter will explore how education must evolve beyond information transfer into conscious transformation. It will examine the necessity of experiential learning and self-inquiry, the role of teachers as facilitators of awareness, and how true education must become a path to awakening, not just a means to employment.

Bridging Intellectual, Emotional, and Spiritual Growth

A human being is not just a thinking mind, he is a being of thought, emotion, and spirit. Education that only develops the intellect but ignores emotional intelligence and spiritual depth creates individuals who are brilliant but disconnected, knowledgeable but directionless, powerful but unfulfilled.

The Bhagavad Gita (2.50) states:

"A person is truly wise when their intellect, emotions, and actions are harmonized. Knowledge alone does not make one complete—it is wisdom in application that matters."

A truly holistic education is one that does not simply fill the mind with knowledge but shapes the entire being, intellect, emotion, and spirit. The first pillar, intellectual growth, aligns with *Jnana Yoga*, the Path of Knowledge. This is the foundation of learning that focuses on the ability to analyze, question, and understand. It is where students engage with theories, literature, scientific discoveries, and complex reasoning. But if education stops here, it creates sharp minds without depth, intelligence without wisdom. Knowledge alone can lead to arrogance if not tempered by something greater.

That is where emotional growth comes in, a principle deeply rooted in *Bhakti Yoga*, the Path of Compassion and Connection. The Upanishads remind us that knowledge without humility is dangerous, and an education system that focuses only on intellectual mastery but ignores human connection produces individuals who may be skilled but lack empathy. A student who excels in debate but does not listen, a leader who strategizes brilliantly but cannot understand the suffering of others, these are the failures of a purely intellectual education. True learning must cultivate kindness, patience, and the ability to see beyond the self.

And finally, there is spiritual growth, the most overlooked yet the most necessary. This aligns with *Dhyana Yoga*, the Path of Inner Awareness, that focuses on the practice of self-inquiry and mindfulness. Without it, education remains outward-focused, teaching students how to succeed in the world but not how to understand themselves. Knowledge must be reflected upon, internalized, and transformed into wisdom. A student who is taught everything except how to sit in stillness and question their own existence is only half-educated. Education, in its truest form, must awaken the mind, open the heart, and deepen the soul, and only then is can be considered as complete.

The great Indian philosopher Swami Vivekananda once said: *"Education is not the amount of information that is put into your brain and runs riot there, undigested, all your life. It is the training by which the will is strengthened, the intellect is expanded, and by which one can stand on one's own feet."*

An education that nourishes only one aspect, intellect, emotion, or spirit, creates imbalance. A scholar without emotional intelligence becomes cold and detached. A person with emotional sensitivity but no intellectual clarity can be misguided. And one who has knowledge and emotion but lacks spiritual grounding may be unable to find true fulfilment. Thus, a true educational system must ensure that students do not just think critically but also feel deeply and introspect profoundly.

Experiential Learning and Self-Inquiry: The Path to Realization

In the Indian spiritual tradition, knowing and realizing are not the same. One fills the mind; the other transforms the being. The Upanishads make this distinction clear by defining two types of knowledge, *Parā Vidyā* and *Aparā Vidyā*.

Parā Vidyā, or Higher Knowledge, is not something that can be memorized or learned from books. It is the kind of wisdom that comes only from direct experience, self-inquiry, and deep realization. It is the difference between reading about fire and actually feeling its heat. A seeker may study scriptures, chant verses, and debate philosophy, but unless the knowledge has been lived, questioned, and internalized, it remains incomplete. *Parā Vidyā* is what leads to true understanding, the realization of the self, the nature of existence, and the wisdom that cannot be forgotten because it is not stored in the mind but embedded in one's consciousness.

In contrast, *Aparā Vidyā*, or Lower Knowledge, is theoretical. It is valuable but limited, the kind of knowledge that fills textbooks, fuels arguments, and wins academic accolades. It is information, not transformation. A scholar may know the entire Bhagavad Gita by heart, but if the words do not shape their actions, if the teachings do not reflect in their choices, they are still trapped in *Aparā Vidyā*. This is the knowledge that helps people build careers, gain expertise, and navigate the material world, but it does not necessarily lead to wisdom.

The greatest mistake modern education makes is assuming that knowing is enough. It celebrates those who can recall facts but does little to cultivate true realization. The Upanishads remind us that knowledge, unless it is lived, is as fleeting as the ink on a page. *Parā Vidyā* liberates; *Aparā Vidyā* only informs. The question is, which one does education truly value today?

This difference is beautifully illustrated in the famous parable of the Salt Doll from Vedantic philosophy.

The Story of the Salt Doll: The Difference Between Knowledge and Experience

A small salt doll wanted to understand the depth of the ocean. It carried books filled with calculations, theories, and measurements. The doll believed that by reading enough, it would know the ocean completely. But when it finally stepped into the water, something unexpected happened, it began to dissolve! As the ocean embraced it, the doll realized that the ocean could never be understood from the shore, it had to be experienced.

The Salt Doll story is a metaphorical tale that illustrates the journey of self-realization and the dissolution of the ego into the infinite. This narrative has been recounted in various spiritual traditions, notably by Ramakrishna Paramahansa, a 19th-century Indian mystic and saint. In his teachings, he used the story to convey the indescribable nature of Brahman (the ultimate reality) and the experience of unity with it. Additionally, the story has been adapted and shared by others, including Anthony de Mello, an East Indian Jesuit priest known for his storytelling that drew from both Eastern and Western mystical traditions. The parable has also been referenced by Swami Vivekananda, who used it to illustrate the concept of the individual soul merging with the absolute.

This crisis in the Salt Doll story can be seen as the fundamental problem with modern education, where students are expected to learn about science, philosophy, and morality through books alone, rather than through experience, reflection, and action.

The Brihadaranyaka Upanishad (4.4.5) states:
"True knowledge is that which is realized through direct experience. Without experience, learning remains incomplete—like a tree without fruit."

A student who reads about gravity but never conducts an experiment, a person who studies art but never picks up a brush, or an individual who reads about ethics but never faces moral dilemmas remains in the realm of theoretical knowledge.

Thus, experiential learning is not a supplement to education, it is education itself.

The Role of Teachers in Awakening Consciousness

A teacher is not just a dispenser of facts but a catalyst for transformation. True education is not about filling minds with knowledge but about awakening the ability to think, question, and realize. The greatest teachers in Indian tradition, Sri Krishna, the Buddha, and Yajnavalkya, did not impose learning upon their students; they illuminated their minds. They understood that knowledge given without inquiry becomes dogma, but knowledge discovered through reflection becomes wisdom.

Let's take Krishna mentorship in the Bhagavad Gita as an example. When Arjun, standing on the battlefield of Kurukshetra, was paralyzed by doubt, Krishna did not give him a simple command. He could have said, *"Pick up your bow and fight,"* but he did not. Instead, he led Arjuna through a process of self-inquiry, challenging his fears, forcing him to confront his emotions, and guiding him toward understanding his own dharma. Krishna did not tell Arjuna what to do—he showed him how to think, how to question his reality, and how to arrive at the truth on his own. Instead of saying *"You must fight,"* Krishna explained why dharma must be upheld. Instead of giving commands, Krishna engaged in philosophical discussion. Instead of feeding blind faith, Krishna cultivated intellectual and spiritual inquiry. This is the hallmark of a true teacher, not to create followers, but to awaken self-reliant thinkers.

The Gautama Buddha's method of teaching followed the same principle. He did not demand that his disciples accept his words without question. Instead, he encouraged deep questioning. When his followers sought answers, he would often respond with another question, leading them to introspect, to challenge their assumptions, to arrive at wisdom not by accepting doctrine but by experiencing truth directly. He famously said, "Do not believe something just because I say it. Test it for yourself." A student asked him once, *"What is truth?"* Instead of answering directly, the Buddha gave him a parable, a story that made the student see the answer for himself rather than be told what to believe. This was the essence of his teaching, not to dictate truth, but to awaken perception.

Another example from our rich ancient mythology is Yajnavalkya, one of the greatest sages of the Upanishads. He also followed this approach. In the *Brihadaranyaka* Upanishad, when his wife, Maitreyi, asked him about the nature of the Self, he did not hand her a ready-made answer. Instead, he led her through a series of reflections, making her see that the ultimate truth was not something to be received from another but something that had to be realized within.

This is the difference between education that liberates and education that enslaves. A poor teacher demands obedience, but a great teacher inspires curiosity. A poor teacher feeds students answers, but a great teacher makes them question. A poor teacher wants students to repeat knowledge, but a great teacher wants them to challenge it, test it, and go beyond it.

Today, many education systems still focus on memorization, compliance, and standardization, rewarding students for how well they remember, rather than how deeply they think. But learning was never meant to be a passive act. The greatest minds in history, from Socrates to Tagore, from Einstein to Vivekananda, all emphasized that true education is about learning how to think, how to question, how to break free from conditioned thought.

A true teacher does not create followers, but thinkers. A true teacher does not impose knowledge, but awakens understanding. A true teacher does not just prepare students for exams—but for life itself.

Hence, if you are simplifying this entire thought and summarising an action plan, then we can say that a true teacher must:

Encourage independent thought rather than passive acceptance.

Cultivate curiosity rather than demanding obedience.

Awaken a student's ability to see beyond textbooks and into life itself.

The Taittiriya Upanishad (1.11.2) says:

"A teacher should not only instruct but embody wisdom, so the student learns through both words and presence."

Teaching as a Path of Awakening

As mentioned earlier, in the modern world, education has become highly structured, assessment-driven, and mechanized. Teachers are often reduced to syllabus-followers, delivering information rather than inspiring inquiry. The classroom that once used to be a space of philosophical debate, ethical reflection, and creative exploration, has been mostly confined to rote learning, standardization, and exam preparation. And why not? Everyone wants tangible outcome-oriented learning. 10th and 12th Board results are considered as quantifies of a student's life and capabilities. Getting into Ivy League colleges are synonymous to a successful life. And thus, to keep up with the demands of the modern-day education system, the teaching-learning methodologies have been modified immensely as well.

But, how far is this race justified? How relevant are these techniques in the long run of life? Can this education system teach students how to be mindful, or how to focus on one's inner self to find peace?

Education in its truest form is not about transferring knowledge, or coaching students to win a race, it is about awakening the student's inner potential. The Bhagavad Gita (4.34) states:

"Approach a true teacher with humility, ask questions, and seek knowledge. The wise who have realized the truth will guide you toward wisdom."

Thus, the role of a teacher is not merely to teach facts but to awaken wisdom. The question is: How can modern educators move beyond being syllabus-driven instructors to becoming facilitators of self-realization?

To answer this, we must explore four essential dimensions of impactful teaching:

1. Cultivating Inquiry Instead of Passive Acceptance
2. Balancing Structure with Freedom
3. Connecting Education to Real-Life and Inner Growth
4. Being a Living Example of Wisdom

Each of these aspects reflects the timeless principles of ancient Indian teaching methods while addressing the needs of contemporary education.

1. Cultivating Inquiry Instead of Passive Acceptance

In most modern classrooms, students are expected to accept information as given. Syllabi are designed in a way that leaves little room for questioning, discussion, or exploration. However, true education begins not when students accept facts, but when they begin to question them.

A great teacher does not merely give answers, he or she stimulates curiosity by asking profound questions. Socrates in the West used his method of dialogue and questioning (Socratic Method) to push students to think for themselves. Krishna in the Bhagavad Gita does not dictate truth to Arjuna. Instead, he engages Arjuna in a series of questions, challenging him to discover the meaning of dharma, duty, and self-knowledge.

When a student questions deeply, they move beyond memorization to genuine understanding.

Now the big question is: How can modern teachers implement this?

To start with, a teacher may, instead of saying: *"This is the law of physics,"* can ask: *"Why do you think nature behaves this way?"*

Or, instead of stating: *"This is the theme of Hamlet,"* can ask: *"If you were Hamlet, what would you have done?"*

Or, instead of telling students what is ethical, the teacher can pose dilemmas and let the students grapple with moral reasoning.

When a classroom becomes a forum for inquiry rather than passive absorption, students are encouraged to think critically, challenge assumptions, and arrive at their own understanding.

As the Chandogya Upanishad (7.1.3) states:
"Knowledge is not in the mere hearing of words, but in the questioning and realization that follows."

2. Balancing Structure with Freedom

Many teachers feel trapped between two extremes, either following a rigid curriculum with no flexibility or allowing complete freedom where learning becomes chaotic. However, the best education strikes a balance between structure and creativity.

Let's look at these examples from the Mahabharata. I will talk about the two great gurus, Dronacharya and Krishna. Dronacharya, the teacher of the Pandavas and Kauravas, emphasized discipline, rigorous practice, and mastery of warfare. His approach was structured and skill-based. Krishna, on the other hand, guided Arjun in an open-ended, philosophical manner. He did not give Arjun strict rules but allowed him to find his own truth through dialogue. Hence, it can be said that a true teacher, a guru, must know when to give structure (like Dronacharya) and when to allow reflection (like Krishna).

So, how can this be implemented in modern teaching methodologies?

Simple. By striking a balance between core lessons and related structured activities, and also by encouraging students to participate in projects, research, and self-driven learning.

Students should also be allowed to choose topics within the curriculum that they can explore independently.

And finally, by creating a classroom culture where mistakes are seen as part of learning rather than as failures.

In the Taittiriya Upanishad (1.11.2), it is said:

"Let the student be guided, but also let them discover. True learning is neither forced nor aimless—it is a harmonious journey."

3. Connecting Education to Real-Life and Inner Growth

A common frustration among students is: "Why am I learning this? How does it matter to my life?" In ancient Indian traditions, education was not separated from real-world applications. The Gurukula system taught Astronomy not just as equations, but as a way to understand nature's rhythms. Mathematics was taught not just as calculations, but as a means to build structures, manage resources, and explore logic. And, Philosophy was not just an abstract theory, but as a way to navigate life's dilemmas.

Let's look at the Story of King Janaka's Education to understand this section better. The *Brihadaranyaka* Upanishad tells the story of King Janaka, who sought the highest wisdom. Many sages gave him philosophical theories, but he remained dissatisfied. Finally, the sage Yajnavalkya told him:

"Wisdom is not in words alone. It must be lived, tested, and realized."

In order to demonstrate this, Yajnavalkya set Janaka's palace on fire. As flames engulfed his kingdom, Janaka remained unmoved, because he had internalized detachment and wisdom. A bit extreme, isn't it? But this is the essence of applied education, it must prepare students not just to pass exams, but to face real challenges in life.

Now the question is how can modern teachers implement this?

First, by relating classroom learning to real-world issues. For example, science to sustainability, history to contemporary society, literature to human psychology. Teachers should teach ethics and decision-making through case studies rather than just textbook definitions. And finally, by encouraging students to engage in social projects, applying their knowledge to solve real problems.

As the Gita (2.50) states:

"The wise act not just with knowledge, but with awareness of its impact on life."

4. Being a Living Example of Wisdom

Perhaps the most important role of a teacher is not in what they teach but who they are. A teacher who is kind, inquisitive, self-aware, and continuously learning inspires students far more than someone who merely gives instructions.

The Guru needs to be a Living Text. But what does this mean?

In Indian tradition, the Guru (teacher) was considered a living embodiment of knowledge. The student did not merely listen to lectures, they observed how the Guru spoke, thought, acted, and lived. If the Guru taught detachment, he must embody detachment in daily life. If the Guru taught compassion, he must practice compassion toward students. If the Guru taught self-discipline, he must exemplify self-discipline in his actions.

But, how relevant is this in the modern times?

I'd say, very much. Learning is a lifelong process, and a teacher, first of all, should continue their own education in some form or the other. A learning teacher creates learning students. Next, emotional intelligence should be modelled in how teachers handle student mistakes, criticism, and challenges. And last but not the least, a teacher should essentially practice to show passion and enthusiasm. When a teacher loves their subject, students feel that energy.

The Mundaka Upanishad (1.2.12) declares:

"The teacher must first embody wisdom before imparting it. For knowledge flows not from words but from being."

Education is timeless, and so are teachers. And hence, a true teacher (guru) should not just teach subjects, but should awaken minds, guide hearts, and inspire souls. And, it is the Modern Gurus who can help the Modern Education move beyond syllabus completion, into a conscious process of inquiry, reflection, and self-discovery.

As Krishna told Arjuna in the Bhagavad Gita (18.63):

"I have given you knowledge. Now, reflect, analyze, and choose your own path."

The greatest teachers do not impose answers, they awaken the student's ability to find them.

But, the question still remains: Are we training teachers to be mere instructors, or are we guiding them to be awakeners of consciousness?

CHAPTER SIX

EDUCATION AS A PATH TO HIGHER CONSCIOUSNESS

The Forgotten Purpose of Learning in the Age of AI

Have you heard the story of Satyakama? Once upon a time, in the ancient kingdom of Videha, a young prince named Satyakama set out in search of true wisdom. Unlike other seekers who pursued kingdoms or wealth, he wished to learn the highest truth, the nature of existence itself. He approached Rishi Gautama, a renowned Guru, and requested to be accepted as a disciple.

The sage asked, *"Who is your father?"*

Satyakama did not know the answer. Raised by his mother, a humble woman named Jabala, he had been taught always to speak the truth. Without hesitation, he replied, *"I do not know my father's name, but my mother has always told me to speak the truth. My name is Satyakama, son of Jabala."*

The sage smiled and said, *"Only a true seeker can answer with such honesty. You are worthy of learning the highest knowledge."*

Under Gautama's guidance, Satyakama did not simply study texts, he lived with nature, observed life deeply, and engaged in inner contemplation. He spent years in self-inquiry, learning from the fire, the wind, and the sky, before finally attaining self-realization.

This story from the *Chandogya* Upanishad is a reminder that education was never meant to be a mere transfer of knowledge, it was meant to be a path to higher consciousness.

Yet, in modern education, we have forgotten this deeper purpose. Schools and universities focus on syllabus completion, exams, and career success, but they do not address the fundamental questions of life - Who am I? Why am I here? What is the meaning of knowledge? This issue is more urgent than ever in the age of Artificial Intelligence (AI). Today, students no longer need to memorize facts, solve equations, or even write essays. AI tools can do all of this for them. With the rise of ChatGPT, AI tutors, and automated learning systems, traditional teaching methods are becoming obsolete.

A student can now use AI-powered apps to solve mathematical equations, generate essays, analyze historical texts, and even create art and music. But is that true education? If information is instantly available, does that mean learning has been achieved?

This brings us to a fundamental question:

What is the purpose of education in a world where knowledge is easily accessible but wisdom is scarce? The answer lies not in technological advancement alone but in returning to the deeper foundations of learning, the ancient systems of holistic education that India once had.

In this chapter, we will explore, the Gurukul System and Wisdom Traditions: How ancient education focused on holistic development. We will talk about transforming the classroom into a place of inner growth: How modern education can integrate higher consciousness, self-inquiry, and experiential learning. And explore the need for a shift in pedagogy in the age of AI: Why today's colonized education system must take inspiration from pre-colonial India's wisdom-based learning models.

First, to understand how education can become a path to awakening, we must first revisit the lost heritage of the Gurukul System and Wisdom Traditions of India and their approach to learning. For centuries, India's education system was one of the most advanced in the world, deeply rooted in self-awareness, experiential learning, and the pursuit of wisdom. Unlike today's classroom-based, standardized, and exam-driven approach, the Gurukul system fostered personalized, holistic, and conscious education that integrated intellectual, emotional, and spiritual development.

The Gurukul system was not just about academics, it was a way of life. It was designed to shape character, awaken intellect, and cultivate self-mastery. The modern education system, shaped largely by colonial influences, has replaced this ancient model with rote learning, mechanical evaluation, and a limited understanding of success.

To understand what we have lost and what we need to reclaim, we must explore:

1. The Origins and Philosophy of the Gurukul System
2. The Structure and Pedagogy of Gurukul Learning
3. The Role of the Guru: The Heart of Conscious Education
4. Great Learning Centers of Ancient India: Takshashila, Nalanda, and Beyond
5. The Decline of Gurukul Education and the Impact of Colonization

Only by revisiting this lost heritage can we understand what modern education lacks and how we can restore learning as a path to higher consciousness.

1. The Origins and Philosophy of the Gurukul System

The word 'Gurukul' comes from two Sanskrit words - 'Guru' (teacher or master) and 'Kul' (family or home). A Gurukul was not just a school, it was the Guru's residence, where students lived as part of an extended family.

Unlike modern institutions, where students attend classes for a few hours and then return home, the Gurukul system immersed students in 24/7 experiential learning. This ensured that education was not a passive activity but an ongoing journey of self-transformation. Even the boarding system of today's times fails to live up to what we had during the Gurukul times.

Now, what really is the Philosophy of Learning in Gurukuls? The foundation of Gurukul education was based on the Vedantic and Upanishadic principles of self-realization and wisdom. The idea was that knowledge is not just external information - it is a path to self-awareness. Learning should be deeply integrated with life, not limited to textbooks. And, true education is not about producing workers but about nurturing enlightened beings.

The Mundaka Upanishad (1.2.12) describes this approach:

"Sa vidya ya vimuktaye" (True education is that which liberates the soul).

This is the greatest contrast between ancient and modern education. Today's education aims to create professionals, while Gurukul education aimed to create enlightened individuals.

2. The Structure and Pedagogy of Gurukul Learning

The pedagogy of Gurukul education was vastly different from modern schools. Instead of standardized exams, rigid curricula, and mechanical learning, Gurukuls followed a personalized, experiential, and wisdom-based approach.

Let's discuss some key Features of Gurukul Learning system.

Personalized Education- Unlike today's one-size-fits-all approach, Gurukuls ensured that each student was taught according to their temperament, abilities, and strengths. If a student was philosophically inclined, he was guided toward the Vedas and Upanishads; if a student was skilled in arts, he was trained in music, sculpture, or poetry.

Experiential Learning Over Rote Memorization- Subjects were not taught in isolation but in an interconnected way. Mathematics was learned through astronomy, language through philosophy, and ethics through real-life applications.

Self-Discipline and Responsibility- Students were responsible for maintaining the Gurukul, cooking, cleaning, and serving their Guru. This was done not as labor but as a means to cultivate humility, responsibility, and detachment from ego.

Learning in Harmony with Nature- Gurukuls were not confined to classrooms but were set in forests and natural surroundings. Students learned by observing the sky, rivers, mountains, and animals, developing a deep respect for the environment.

The Story of Aruni's Dedication to Learning

In order to provide a little clarity t these ideas, I would like to discuss a famous story from the Mahabharata highlights the self-discipline and experiential learning of Gurukul students. One evening, Aruni, a devoted student of Rishi Dhoumya, noticed that the fields near the Gurukul were flooding due to a broken embankment. Understanding the urgency of the situation, he laid his own body across the gap to stop the water flow. The next morning, when the Guru found him in this state, he said:

"Aruni, your learning is complete. You have understood that knowledge is not just in books but in action, sacrifice, and wisdom."

This was the true essence of Gurukul learning - students did not just read about values; they lived them.

3. The Role of the Guru

Gurus are the hearts of conscious education. Unlike today, where teachers are seen as instructors, Gurukuls viewed the Guru as a spiritual guide and mentor. The Guru's role was not just to transfer knowledge but to awaken wisdom. Let's discuss what made Gurus different from modern teachers?

They Led by Example- A Guru was not just a source of information but a living embodiment of wisdom. The Taittiriya Upanishad (1.11.2) states:

"A teacher must first embody wisdom before imparting it to students."

They Encouraged Deep Inquiry- Instead of dictating answers, Gurus engaged in dialogue and questioning. This was the Socratic method centuries before Socrates!

They Focused on Character Building- A student's moral development was considered more important than academic achievements. The Bhagavad Gita (4.34) describes the importance of the Guru:

"Approach a true teacher with humility, ask questions, and seek wisdom. The realized ones will guide you toward truth." Today, where teachers are often reduced to syllabus-followers, this Guru-student bond is desperately needed.

4. Great Learning Centers of Ancient India

India's ancient universities, Takshashila, Nalanda, Vikramashila, and Vallabhi, were global centers of learning long before modern universities.

Takshashila (4th Century BCE – 5th Century CE) is the world's first known university, attracting students from Greece, Persia, China, and Arabia. Subjects taught here ranged from Vedic scriptures to mathematics, logic, medicine, and political science.

Nalanda (5th Century – 12th Century CE) hosted over 10,000 students and 2,000 teachers. The university was known for debates, logic, and Buddhist philosophy. These universities followed Gurukul principles, proving that India's education was far superior to rote-learning-based models.

5. The Origin of Modern Education in India and the Loss of True Learning

In the early 19th century, when the British solidified their control over India, they realized that to govern such a vast and diverse land, they needed a structured administrative workforce. However, there was a problem. India already had a thriving, decentralized, and deeply philosophical education system rooted in Gurukuls, pathshalas, and centers of higher learning like Nalanda and Takshashila. This system did not produce obedient clerks but rather independent thinkers, spiritual seekers, scientists, and philosophers. In order to break this model and replace it with one that would serve their own interests, the British, under Lord Macaulay, introduced a Western education policy that focused on producing English-speaking clerks and government officers rather than intellectuals, philosophers, or visionaries. In 1835, Macaulay famously stated:

"A single shelf of a good European library is worth the whole native literature of India and Arabia."

This statement was not just an insult to India's heritage, it was a carefully planned strategy to disconnect Indians from their spiritual and intellectual roots, making them more dependent on British rule. The education system that followed was designed to strip Indians of their deep-rooted wisdom, replacing it with a mechanical, exam-oriented model that remains in place even today.

The result?

Education became synonymous with job security rather than self-discovery. Colonized minds began to believe that Indian knowledge systems were outdated. The philosophical and holistic approach to learning that once defined Indian education was abandoned for a Western, industrialized model.

This shift was not just an educational loss, it was a spiritual loss. The Bhagavad Gita, Upanishads, and other ancient texts that once formed the foundation of learning were replaced by a rigid syllabus, mechanical memorization, and a focus on producing obedient employees rather than awakened individuals.

Yet, even during this era of colonization, a few visionaries saw the damage being done and sought to revive India's lost educational wisdom. Two such figures were Swami Vivekananda and Rabindranath Tagore, both of whom recognized the need to reclaim India's rich intellectual and spiritual traditions and fought against the colonized system of learning.

Swami Vivekananda: The Messenger of India's Lost Wisdom

In 1893, a young monk from India stood before the World's Parliament of Religions in Chicago and changed the way the world saw Indian wisdom forever. Swami Vivekananda, dressed in saffron robes, with a calm but powerful presence, addressed an audience that was largely unfamiliar with the depth of India's spiritual and educational heritage.

He began with the words:

"Sisters and brothers of America."

This single phrase, not "ladies and gentlemen," but "sisters and brothers", was not just a greeting; it was a profound expression of the Indian worldview. It was the very philosophy that the ancient Indian Education system once embodied, that knowledge is not merely for personal gain, but for the upliftment of humanity. Vivekananda spoke about Vedantic philosophy, the Upanishads, and the essence of education as self-realization. He reminded the world that India had always been a land of seekers, where education was not confined to classrooms but was an inward journey of self-discovery. He said:

"Education is the manifestation of perfection already in man."

For him, education was not about filling a child's mind with information but about drawing out the innate potential that already exists within. This was the Indian way of learning where a student was not treated as an empty vessel but as a soul waiting to be awakened. His speeches were met with overwhelming applause, respect, and admiration. The West, which had long dismissed India as a land of mysticism and superstition, now saw it as a repository of profound wisdom. And yet, back in India, the very education system that had once produced such wisdom was being dismantled.

Swami Vivekananda's call was clear: India must return to its roots. It must rediscover its lost education system, one that was built not on producing workers but on producing enlightened individuals.

Rabindranath Tagore: Building a New Model of Education at Santiniketan

While Vivekananda traveled the world spreading India's spiritual message, another great mind, Rabindranath Tagore, was deeply troubled by the state of education in India. Born into a family of scholars, Tagore saw firsthand how colonial education was stifling creativity, free thinking, and the pursuit of knowledge beyond exams. Unlike the ancient Indian education system, which embraced open-air learning, artistic exploration, and philosophical inquiry, the British model was rigid, confining, and disconnected from nature and self-reflection. Tagore rejected this system and instead created Santiniketan - a place where students would learn not in closed classrooms but under the open sky, in harmony with nature, and in the spirit of inquiry rather than forced memorization.

He envisioned an education that was rooted in Indian philosophy, yet open to the world. An education that was artistic, poetic, and deeply connected to creativity. A system that was not exam-driven, but exploration-driven.

At Santiniketan, students read the Upanishads under the shade of trees, composed poetry, painted, and engaged in discussions that had no rigid syllabus but infinite intellectual freedom.

Tagore famously said:

"The highest education is that which does not merely give us information but makes our life in harmony with all existence."

This was a direct challenge to the colonized system of education, which was designed to make students followers rather than thinkers. Santiniketan was a modern revival of the Gurukul system, a model that prioritized self-expression, wisdom, and cultural pride over mechanical learning.

Tagore and Vivekananda, though working in different ways, were both saying the same thing:

India must reclaim its lost educational wisdom.

The Need for a Return to Ancient Knowledge in the Age of AI

Today, as we enter an era dominated by Artificial Intelligence (AI) and digital automation, the need to redefine education is greater than ever. Students can now use AI to generate essays, solve complex equations, and even compose poetry. But does this mean they are truly educated?

AI can provide information, but it cannot provide wisdom.

If education is reduced to memorization and skill acquisition, then AI will surpass humans in every way. But if education is about self-discovery, ethical reasoning, and the pursuit of higher consciousness, then no AI can replace the human mind and spirit.

This is why it is time to look back to our past to create a better future. The Gurukul system, the Vedantic traditions, and the educational models of thinkers like Vivekananda and Tagore hold the answers to what education must become in this age of automation. Education must once again focus on consciousness, not just content.

The Brihadaranyaka Upanishad (4.4.5) states:
"True knowledge is that which leads to the realization of the self."

And this is the question we must ask:

Are we still following a system designed to produce clerks for a foreign empire, or are we ready to build an education system that awakens the soul, sharpens the mind, and elevates human consciousness? For in the end, reiterating the same, education should not just create workers, it should create awakened beings.

Transforming the Classroom into a Place of Inner Growth

The challenge of modern education is not lack of information but lack of meaning. Students study without knowing why, they prepare for exams without understanding their relevance, and they pursue careers without self-awareness.

For classrooms to become places of true learning, they must become spaces of intellectual expansion, emotional intelligence, and self-inquiry.

Let this question reverberate: Why AI Cannot Replace True Education?

The answer, although known to us, needs to be restated and reiterated over and over again so that we do not forget the reason why true education is important and our ancient education system is still relevant today. AI can generate knowledge, but it cannot cultivate wisdom. AI can write poetry, but it cannot experience emotions. AI can predict historical patterns, but it cannot grasp ethical dilemmas. And, this is why human-led education must evolve, integrating elements of self-awareness, ethics, and spiritual understanding that AI cannot replicate.

Everything said, if you are still wondering how can we apply ancient learning methods today? Let me guide you with a simpler understanding.

Our modern education system should be encouraging Self-Inquiry and Reflection. Instead of focusing only on grades and exams, schools must teach introspection, debate, and ethical reasoning.

We should also integrate Mindfulness and Conscious Learning. Not just Social-Emotion Learning Classes (SEL), but more. Just as Gurukuls integrated meditation and silence, modern education must include mindfulness practices to improve attention and awareness. Teachers and education institutions should encourage Learning by Doing, not just consuming information. Experiential projects, research, and real-world learning should be prioritized over memorization.

The Bhagavad Gita (3.35) reminds us:
"It is better to follow one's own path imperfectly than to imitate another's perfectly."

A true classroom should not just be a place of knowledge, it should be a space for discovering one's dharma (true purpose).

It is not wrong to say that with so many national and international curricula in place, and so many diverse pedagogies to choose from, the education system is at a crossroads. On one hand, technology is advancing rapidly, and on the other, humanity is losing touch with the deeper purpose of learning. And, this is where the ancient India's wisdom traditions provide a blueprint for integrating AI-driven education with spiritual depth and self-awareness, so that we may collectively emerge as a nation of true greatness once again.

The Brihadaranyaka Upanishad (4.4.5) states:
"True knowledge is that which leads to the realization of the self."

Thus, it can be said that the future of education is not just about more advanced AI or better exams, it is about ensuring that students do not just know more but become more. It is time that every educator should ask themselves: Are we preparing students for a world of information, or are we guiding them toward a world of wisdom?

CHAPTER SEVEN

CONCLUSION, OR IS IT?

A Call for Change – From Shikshaks to Gurus

For centuries, education in India was a sacred journey of transformation, designed not just to produce knowledgeable individuals but to create conscious beings. It was not a system of rote learning or standardized exams but a path toward higher awareness, self-discovery, and wisdom. From the Gurukul traditions to the teachings of the Bhagavad Gita, from the philosophy of Swami Vivekananda to the educational reforms of Rabindranath Tagore, India has always stood as a beacon of intellectual and spiritual enlightenment. Yet, today, we stand at a critical crossroads in history.

The education system that once nurtured seekers, innovators, and philosophers has been replaced by an industrialized model, one that prioritizes grades over growth, careers over character, and compliance over curiosity. This transition was not accidental; it was a deliberate shift imposed during British colonization, designed to produce obedient workers rather than independent thinkers. As we have seen in earlier chapters, Lord Macaulay's education policy systematically dismantled India's knowledge traditions, replacing them with a rigid, Western-centric system that still dominates our classrooms today.

And now, in the 21st century, we face another disruption, the rise of Artificial Intelligence (AI) and digital automation, which threatens to further strip education of its essence.

In the previous chapters, we explored: The wisdom of ancient education systems (Chapter 1 & 2), where learning was holistic, experiential, and deeply rooted in self-inquiry. The distinction between true wisdom and mechanical learning (Chapter 3 & 4), using Bloom's Taxonomy and Gurdjieff's philosophy to show how real education moves beyond memorization into higher consciousness. The colonization of Indian education (Chapter 5 & 6), which replaced self-awareness with industrial training, stripping learning of its deeper purpose.

Now, as we conclude this discussion, we must ask ourselves: What is the future of education? How do we reclaim our lost wisdom while embracing the new realities of AI and digital learning?

The answer lies in a call for change, a transformation from being shikshaks (instructors) to Gurus (guides of wisdom and consciousness).

A highly debated topic in today's world is the impact of AI on our future - whether it is a threat or an opportunity. The same debate extends to the future of education as well. For centuries, education was about acquiring knowledge, but now, machines can do that faster and better than us. AI can solve equations, generate essays, analyze historical events, and even predict future trends. With tools like ChatGPT, AI tutors, and automated learning platforms, students can now memorize and reproduce information effortlessly. But here lies the paradox - if AI can do everything that traditional education trains students to do, then what is the purpose of human learning? If knowledge alone defines intelligence, then AI is already more intelligent than us. But if intelligence is defined by wisdom, self-awareness, and higher consciousness, then machines will never surpass us.

This is why we need a radical shift in our approach to education. AI should not be feared; it should be embraced. But embracing AI does not mean surrendering to it. It means using technology to free ourselves from repetitive tasks so that we can focus on higher learning, creativity, and self-inquiry.

A New Model of Education for the Future

The education system we need now must be fundamentally different from the industrialized, exam-driven model of the past. It must return to the wisdom of the Gurukul system, the insights of ancient philosophy, and the self-inquiry methods of thinkers like Gurdjieff.

Gurdjieff taught that most people live in a state of 'mechanical consciousness', trapped in repetitive thought patterns, behaving like machines rather than conscious beings. He argued that true education is the process of 'waking up' from this cycle. This is exactly what India's ancient wisdom traditions have always emphasized, learning is not just about knowing; it is about becoming. We must remember that AI can calculate, but it cannot contemplate. AI can write, but it cannot create with emotion and depth. AI can store knowledge, but it cannot seek truth. Thus, the role of education is no longer just to teach facts but to cultivate wisdom, the ability to think critically, analyze ethically, create meaningfully, and live consciously. To achieve this, we, as educators, must transform our roles.

From Shikshaks to Gurus: The Responsibility of Educators

For too long, teachers have been reduced to syllabus-followers, taskmasters, and exam supervisors. The system rewards those who teach to the test rather than those who awaken minds. But now, we must rise beyond this outdated model.

The true responsibility of an educator is not to produce workers but to cultivate awakened human beings. A true teacher does not just transfer knowledge, they ignite curiosity, instil wisdom, and guide students toward self-realization.

The big question is how can we become Gurus in the Age of AI?

The answer is simpler than ever. We need to encourage Inquiry Over Memorization. Moving beyond textbooks, we need to ask students to reflect, analyze, and debate rather than just recall facts. We need to teach students to question everything, including AI-generated answers.

As educators of modern times, we must incorporate Experiential and Self-Inquiry Learning. By using real-world projects, ethical dilemmas, and creative challenges, we need to help students engage with learning on a deeper level. We also need to integrate meditation, self-reflection, and mindfulness practices to cultivate awareness beyond academics.

It is a must that we teach Ethical and Conscious Use of AI to our students. AI should be a tool, not a crutch. Students must learn to use AI responsibly, ethically, and creatively. Instead of fearing AI, we must teach students to do what AI cannot, think critically, empathize deeply, and live meaningfully.

It is time that we reclaim India's lost Wisdom Traditions. It is time that we incorporate teachings from the Upanishads, the Bhagavad Gita, and Vedantic philosophy to provide students with spiritual and ethical grounding. This has nothing to do with religion, as life skills based on spiritual philosophy has no limitations or restrictions. We should also try to revive the essence of Gurukul model where education is not just about skills but about self-mastery.

Another important aspect that today's educators should do: develop character of the students alongside intelligence. The Bhagavad Gita (2.50) teaches that a wise person harmonizes knowledge, action, and devotion. An educator should teach students that success is not just about achievements but about becoming better human beings.

The Future of Education - A Call to Action

The Bhagavad Gita (18.63) states:
"I have given you knowledge. Now, reflect, analyze, and choose your own path."

This is our moment to choose. We can continue following the colonized, industrialized model of education, producing students who are technically skilled but spiritually empty, knowledgeable but unaware of themselves. Or, we can reclaim the lost heritage of true education—one that integrates wisdom, self-awareness, and higher consciousness into learning. This is not just an institutional change - it is a shift in mindset. It begins with us, the educators.

We must become Gurus, not just teachers.

We must create seekers, not just students.

We must awaken minds, not just fill them.

The future of education is not about competing with AI, it is about ensuring that even as technology advances, we never lose sight of what makes us truly human. For in the end, education is not just about knowing more - it is about becoming more.

The question is no longer: What will students learn?
The question is: What kind of human beings will they become?

The choice is ours. The time for change is now.

Author's Note

Dear Readers,

Fifteen years. That's how long I've been in the world of education - teaching, mentoring, counseling, training teachers, and navigating the administrative labyrinths of different schools across different cities in India. And no matter where I went, it was more or less the same story. The same race for marks, the same syllabus-driven monotony, the same westernized system repackaged under new terminologies. I've seen it from every possible perspective, standing in front of a classroom, sitting across from anxious students in counseling sessions, and from behind a desk in school leadership meetings. And no matter the vantage point, one thing became painfully clear: we are recycling an outdated education model that does little to awaken real learning.

We attend professional development programs, complete rigorous teacher training, and sit through hours of "innovative pedagogy" workshops, only to realize that it's the same Western frameworks being taught to us in loops, wrapped in fancy jargon. Bloom's Taxonomy, 21st-century skills, inquiry-based learning - yes, they all have merit. But why are we still ignoring the vast, rich educational heritage that India has nurtured for thousands of years?

I am not here to reject Western models - far from it. Education is universal, and learning from different systems is essential. But what I am questioning is our blind dependence on them while we completely sideline our own indigenous wisdom. The Gurukul system, the Upanishadic way of learning, the Wisdom Tradition, the holistic approach of Indian pedagogy - these were not just effective; they were transformative. They didn't just produce professionals; they nurtured thinkers, leaders, visionaries. Why is that not the need of the hour today?

This book is my way of asking that question. Not just as an educator, but as someone who has lived through the system, questioned it, and seen its cracks firsthand. Through my experiences, my research, and my relentless curiosity about what education could and should be, I have tried to pen down a wake-up call. Because that's what we, as educators, need - a rude awakening.

We cannot keep tinkering around the edges of a broken system. We need bold, foundational changes. And that starts with recognizing, reclaiming, and reintroducing our own educational heritage, not as an archaic relic of the past, but as a solution for the future.

To every teacher, administrator, policymaker, and changemaker reading this - I hope this book shakes you up a little. I hope it makes you rethink. And most of all, I hope it makes you question whether we are truly preparing our students for the future, or just dragging them through an outdated past.

With Love,
Aindrila

About The Author

Aindrila Ghosal, born in Kolkata, studied Comparative Literature at Jadavpur University and has spent 15 years in academia as a teacher, counselor, and education leader. She currently works in an international school in Hyderabad. An avid reader and relentless researcher, she believes that true education lies not in acceptance, but in the courage to seek, challenge, and transform.

Author: Aindrila Ghosal

Citations And Sources

Chapter 1

Primary Sources
The Bhagavad Gita
Translation by Swami Sivananda (2000).
Bhagavad Gita 2.50: "A wise person harmonizes knowledge, action, and devotion. Only then does life become meaningful."
The Upanishads
Brihadaranyaka Upanishad (4.4.5): "True knowledge is that which is realized through direct experience. Without experience, learning remains incomplete—like a tree without fruit."
Taittiriya Upanishad (1.11.2): "A teacher should inspire not just with words but by being a living example of wisdom."
Mundaka Upanishad (1.2.12)
"Education must liberate the soul."
Secondary Sources
Radhakrishnan, S. (1953). The Principal Upanishads. Harper & Brothers.
Dasgupta, S. (1922). A History of Indian Philosophy, Vol 1. Cambridge University Press.

Chapter 2

Primary Sources
Samkhya Philosophy
Kapila's Teachings in Samkhya Karika: "The distinction between smriti (memory-based knowledge) and buddhi (intellect-based knowledge) is key to true wisdom."
The Bhagavad Gita
Gita 4.18: "He who sees action in inaction, and inaction in action, is truly wise."

Katha Upanishad

Story of Nachiketa: Translated by Swami Vivekananda in Complete Works of Swami Vivekananda, Vol 1 (1897).

Secondary Sources

Radhakrishnan, S. (1948). Indian Philosophy, Vol 1. Oxford University Press.

Vivekananda, Swami. (1893). Lectures on Vedanta Philosophy. Ramakrishna Mission.

Chapter 3

Primary Sources

Bloom, B. S. (1956). Taxonomy of Educational Objectives: The Classification of Educational Goals.

The Upanishads

Chandogya Upanishad (7.1.3): "Knowledge is not in the mere hearing of words, but in the questioning and realization that follows."

The Bhagavad Gita

Gita 3.35: "It is better to follow one's own path imperfectly than to imitate another's perfectly."

The Story of Karna and Arjuna (Mahabharata, Critical Edition, Bhandarkar Oriental Research Institute, Pune)

Secondary Sources

Shankaracharya, A. (c. 9th century). Commentary on Bhagavad Gita.

Bhattacharya, R. (2011). The Samkhya Philosophy: A Study of Its Origin and Development. Routledge.

Chapter 4

Primary Sources

The Upanishads

Taittiriya Upanishad (1.11.2): "Education must develop not just intelligence but wisdom. It must lead not just to learning but to realization."

The Bhagavad Gita

Gita 2.50: "A wise person harmonizes knowledge, action, and devotion. Only then does life become meaningful."

Gita 4.34: "Approach a true teacher with humility, ask questions, and seek knowledge. The wise who have realized the truth will guide you toward wisdom."

The Story of King Janaka and Yajnavalkya

Brihadaranyaka Upanishad, translated by Radhakrishnan (1953).

Secondary Sources

Swami Vivekananda. (1893). World's Parliament of Religions Lectures.

Tagore, R. (1917). Personality: Lectures Delivered in America. Macmillan.

Dasgupta, S. (1940). A History of Indian Philosophy, Vol 3. Cambridge University Press.

Chapter 5

Primary Sources

The Bhagavad Gita

Gita 18.63: "I have given you knowledge. Now, reflect, analyze, and choose your own path."

The Story of Satyakama Jabala

Chandogya Upanishad (4.4.5), translated by Swami Sivananda.

The Story of Aruni and Rishi Dhoumya

Mahabharata, Critical Edition, Bhandarkar Oriental Research Institute, Pune.

Mundaka Upanishad (1.2.12)

"Education must liberate the soul."

Secondary Sources

Tagore, R. (1929). The Religion of Man. Macmillan.

Vivekananda, Swami. (1893). Addresses at the Parliament of Religions. Ramakrishna Mission.

Sharma, A. (2002). Ancient Indian Education: Brahmanical and Buddhist. Motilal Banarsidass.

Chapter 6

Primary Sources

G.I. Gurdjieff's Teachings

Gurdjieff, G. I. (1949). Beelzebub's Tales to His Grandson. Penguin Books.

Gurdjieff, G. I. (1950). Meetings with Remarkable Men. Routledge.

The Bhagavad Gita

Gita 18.63: "I have given you knowledge. Now, reflect, analyze, and choose your own path."

Gita 2.50: "Education should create awakened beings, not just knowledgeable individuals."

AI and Education

Tegmark, M. (2017). Life 3.0: Being Human in the Age of Artificial Intelligence. Knopf.

Kurzweil, R. (2005). The Singularity is Near: When Humans Transcend Biology. Viking.

Secondary Sources

Robinson, K. (2011). Out of Our Minds: Learning to Be Creative. Wiley.

Sharma, Y. (2021). Reimagining Indian Education in the 21st Century. Sage Publications.

General Sources Used Across Chapters

Macaulay, T. B. (1835). Minutes on Indian Education.

Mahatma Gandhi (1937). The Story of My Experiments with Truth. Navajivan Trust.

Sri Aurobindo (1920). National Education in India. Arya Publishing.

Tagore, R. (1917). My School. Visva-Bharati.

Radhakrishnan, S. (1953). The Principal Upanishads. Harper & Brothers.

Dasgupta, S. (1922). A History of Indian Philosophy, Vol 1. Cambridge University Press.

Therigatha (Verses of the Elder Nuns), Therigatha 2.3

This text, part of the Pali Canon, records the verses of enlightened Buddhist nuns, including Khema's realization of impermanence and wisdom.

Dhammapada Commentary (DhA 11.6)

The commentary on the Dhammapada recounts how Khema, proud of her beauty, was transformed by Buddha's teachings, realizing that youth and beauty fade but wisdom is eternal.

Anguttara Nikaya (AN 1.14.5)

Mentions Khema as one of the two foremost female disciples of Buddha (the other being Uppalavanna), highlighting her wisdom and deep understanding of the Dharma.

Bloom, B. S. (1956). Taxonomy of Educational Objectives: The Classification of Educational Goals. Longmans, Green.

Easwaran, E. (1985). The Bhagavad Gita for Daily Living. Nilgiri Press.

Mundaka Upanishad, 1.1.5, Sacred Books of the East, Vol. 15.

Vivekananda, S. (1893). The Complete Works of Swami Vivekananda. Advaita Ashrama.

Einstein, A., & Tagore, R. (1930). Conversation on Truth and Reality, Berlin.

Dutta, K., & Robinson, A. (1995). Rabindranath Tagore: The Myriad-Minded Man. Bloomsbury.

Holton, G. (1971). Einstein, History, and Other Passions: The Rebellion Against Science at the End of the Twentieth Century. Harvard University Press.

Citations for Maslow's Limitations

Maslow, A. H. (1969). The Farther Reaches of Human Nature. Journal of Transpersonal Psychology, 1(1), 1-9.

In this work, Maslow acknowledges that self-actualization is not the highest stage of human development and introduces the concept of self-transcendence, which aligns more closely with Eastern spiritual traditions.

Koltko-Rivera, M. E. (2006). Rediscovering the Later Version of Maslow's Hierarchy of Needs: Self-Transcendence and Opportunities for Theory, Research, and Unification. Review of General Psychology, 10(4), 302-317.

This paper discusses how Maslow, toward the end of his life, revised his hierarchy to include self-transcendence, showing that his original model was incomplete.

Frick, W. B. (1983). The Transcendent Dimension of Personhood. Journal of Humanistic Psychology, 23(3), 13-26.

A deeper exploration of Maslow's later work, explaining why his final thoughts on human development leaned toward Eastern spirituality, particularly concepts found in Vedanta and Buddhism.

Citations for Advaita Vedanta's Principles

Shankara, A. (circa 8th century). Vivekachudamani (Crest-Jewel of Discrimination). Trans. Swami Prabhavananda & Christopher Isherwood, Vedanta Press, 1978.

One of the most important texts of Advaita Vedanta, this book discusses the illusion of self, the need to dissolve ego, and the ultimate realization of oneness with Brahman.

Deutsch, E. (1969). Advaita Vedanta: A Philosophical Reconstruction. University of Hawaii Press.

This book provides a modern academic interpretation of Advaita Vedanta, discussing how self-actualization is an illusion because the self itself is an illusion.

Radhakrishnan, S. (1953). The Principal Upanishads. Harper & Brothers.

A foundational work on Upanishadic philosophy, explaining how human fulfillment is not about achieving personal greatness but about dissolving individuality into the universal self (Brahman).

Eliot, C. (1921). Hinduism and Buddhism: An Historical Sketch, Vol. 3. Routledge.

Discusses how Western psychology (including Maslow's ideas) tends to focus on personal fulfillment, whereas Indian philosophy focuses on the dissolution of personal identity itself.